D1602659

ORIGINAL
UNITY
of MAN
and WOMAN

*Catechesis on the
Book of Genesis*

ORIGINAL UNITY of MAN and WOMAN

Catechesis on the Book of Genesis

JOHN PAUL II

Preface by Donald W. Wuerl

ST. PAUL EDITIONS

Reprinted with permission of *L'Osservatore Romano*, English Edition.

Library of Congress Cataloging in Publication Data

John Paul II, Pope, 1920-
      Original unity of man and woman.

    1. Marriage—Moral and religious aspects—Catholic Church—
Meditations. 2. Man (Christian theology)—Biblical teaching
—Meditations. 3. Bible. O.T. Genesis I-III—Meditations.
I. Daughters of St. Paul. II. Title.

BX2250.J64   261.8'358   81-9078
ISBN 0-8198-5405-0   AACR2
ISBN 0-8198-5406-0 (pbk.)

Printed in U.S.A. by the Daughters of St. Paul
50 St. Paul's Ave., Boston, MA 02130

The Daughters of St. Paul are an international congregation
of religious women serving the Church with the
communications media.

CONTENTS

Preface

We are well into the second century of the age of progress—modern times—as we sometimes hear it called. For many the scientific and industrial revolutions that started in Europe over 100 years ago were the beginning of a new world order—the Genesis of a new creation.

Science was producing wonderful and potentially powerful new ideas that were not only providing additional information about nature, but were actually creating whole new fields: bacteriology, atomic physics, genetics, psychology, anthropology, and sociology. Science had even invented a new method of invention: applied science. All of these developments strengthened a vision that through the discovery and application of new scientific data human beings could bring the world and mankind itself under human mastery and achieve an earthly paradise. For many during the last century science replaced religion and philosophy as the standard of hope and welfare.

The useful took the place of the beautiful. Industry stepped in where once art had flourished. Political economy was the surrogate of religion and arithmetic displaced poetry.

The heirs of this view of life can add countless scientific triumphs to the long list of human technological progress—space walks, moon landings, miracle drugs, instantaneous communications systems—and a host of other benefits.

Yet beneath all this foliage of progress are the thorns of human discontent. Heartaches, loneliness, betrayal, egoism, hatred, and alienation still seem to flourish and even flower. The human spirit does not seem to be either calmed or satisfied by all the material progress that soothes our bodies and calms our physical needs.

To what do we owe this unsettling distance between physical comfort and spiritual peace? What name do we give the fact of our human experience that says not all goes well—even if the great riches of science are ours?

The great men and women of our ancestors on this planet searched with equal vigor and frustration for some answer to the perplexing nature of human life and contentment. What recorded history we have in the form of ancient writings is laced with this human riddle. Who are we? What should we do? How should we live? What answer do we make to the dilemma of human frailty and failure in the light of so much human potential and promise? Wherein lies the clue that unlocks the mystery of human greatness, petty selfishness, startling progress and constant saneness?

The Book of Genesis looks at this troublesome question. It is the story of man and woman's reflection—under the inspiration of God—on our human condition. With a timelessness born of repeated human experience this first book of the Bible confronts the gnawing demand: How can what is so good contain so much that turns out bad?

Jean Jacques Rousseau once wrote, "Man is born free and is everywhere in chains." His observation is equally applicable to the world of the soul—the realm of human spiritual greatness. Why with so much love is there also such abundance of sin?

In turning his attention to the Book of Genesis, Pope John Paul II singles out one particular aspect of the human condition that seems forever destined to be a cause of great joy and profound sorrow—marriage. The theme of this book is set by the subject of the talks given by the Holy Father to general audiences from September 5, 1979, through April 2, 1980. During this time he has concentrated on the mystery of man and woman as God created them and the union in marriage of the two as He intended it. The meditations have a timeless ring to them as do the questions he raises.

As I sat in the audience hall during one of these conferences my mind wandered to the large crowd—some 9,000 people who filled every seat in the huge Pope Paul VI Aula. Like myself, most of those visitors had come to glimpse the Holy Father, hear his voice, join him in prayer and receive his encouragement and blessing. It is hard in such circumstances of excitement, enthusiasm and joy to concentrate entirely on the depth of the message being

voiced by the Pope. This is all the more aggravated by the need to be present for so long a
meditation in piecemeal fashion over a long
series of audiences. I was hearing only one part
of what was intended to be a long commentary.
And so I had the feeling I was really hearing
only one chapter of a much larger book.

Thanks to the Daughters of St. Paul the rest
of the chapters of that same book are now
available between two covers. *Catechesis on
the Book of Genesis* presents the complete texts
of the Holy Father's commentary on Genesis as
it evolved in his Wednesday general audience
talks. The importance of these reflections is
obvious to any observer of the human condition
today.

One word of warning to the reader. These
talks are not after dinner speeches filled with
humorous anecdotes. They are very serious
meditations on a difficult Book of the Bible. This
collection of talks by the Holy Father requires
considerable attention, both during and after
reading. Another word of gratitude, this time to
the Daughters of St. Paul for making available
to all of us this needed and marvelous collection
of insightful reflections by our Holy Father.

Donald W. Wuerl

Unity and Indissolubility of Marriage

General audience, September 5, 1979.

1. For some time now preparations have been going on for the next ordinary assembly of the Synod of Bishops, which will take place in Rome in autumn of next year. The theme of the Synod: *De muneribus familiae christianae* (The role of the Christian family) concentrates our attention on this community of human and Christian life, which has been fundamental *from the beginning*. The Lord Jesus used precisely this expression *"from the beginning"* in the talk about marriage, reported in the Gospel of St. Matthew and that of St. Mark. We wish to raise the question what this word: "beginning" means. We also wish to clarify why Christ refers to the "beginning" precisely on that occasion and, therefore, we propose a more precise analysis of the relative text of Holy Scripture.

CLEAR-CUT RESPONSES

2. Twice, during the talk with the Pharisees, who asked Him the question about the indissolubility of marriage, Jesus Christ referred to the "beginning." The talk took place in the following way:

"...And Pharisees came up to him and tested him by asking, 'Is it lawful to divorce one's wife for any cause?' He answered, 'Have you not read that he who made them from the beginning made them male and female, and said, 'For this reason a man shall leave his father and mother and be joined to his wife, and the two shall become one flesh'? So they are no longer two but one flesh. What therefore God has joined together, let not man put asunder.' They said to him, 'Why then did Moses command one to give a certificate of divorce, and to put her away?' He said to them, 'For your hardness of heart Moses allowed you to divorce your wives, *but from the beginning it was not so*' " (Mt. 19:3ff. cf. also Mk. 10:2ff.).

Christ does not accept the discussion at the level at which His interlocutors try to introduce it; in a certain sense He does not approve of the dimension that they have tried to give the problem. He avoids getting caught up in juridico-casuistical controversies; and on the contrary He refers twice to "the beginning." Acting in this way, He makes a clear reference to the relative words in the book of Genesis, which His interlocutors too know by heart. From those words of the ancient revelation, Christ draws the conclusion and the talk ends.

FROM THE BEGINNING

3. "The beginning" means, therefore, that which the book of Genesis speaks about. It is, therefore, Genesis 1:27 that Christ quotes, in summary form: "In the beginning the Creator made them male and female," while the original passage reads textually as follows: "God created man in his own image, in the image of God he created him; male and female he created them." Subsequently, the Master refers to Genesis 2:24: "Therefore, a man leaves his father and his mother and cleaves to his wife, and they become one flesh." Quoting these words almost "in extenso," in full, Christ gives them an even more explicit normative meaning (since it could be supported that in the Book of *Genesis* they express *de facto* statements: "leaves...cleaves...they become one flesh"). The normative meaning is plausible since Christ does not confine Himself only to the quotation itself, but adds: "So they are no longer two but one flesh. What therefore God has joined together, let not man put asunder." That "let not man put asunder" is decisive. In the light of these words of Christ, Genesis 2:24 sets forth the principle of the unity and indissolubility of marriage as the very content of the Word of God, expressed in the most ancient revelation.

THE ETERNAL LAW

4. It could be maintained at this point that the problem is exhausted, that Jesus Christ's words confirm the eternal law formulated and set up by God from "the beginning" as the creation of man. It might also seem that the Master, confirming this original law of the Creator, does nothing but establish exclusively his own normative meaning, referring to the authority itself of the first Legislator. However, that significant expression: "from the beginning," repeated twice, clearly induces his interlocutors to reflect on the way in which man was formed in the mystery of creation, precisely as "male and female," in order to understand correctly the normative sense of the words of Genesis. And this is no less valid for the interlocutors of today than for those of that time. Therefore, in the present study, considering all this, we must put ourselves precisely in the position of Christ's interlocutors today.

PREPARATION FOR THE SYNOD

5. During the following Wednesday reflections, at the general audiences, we will try, as Christ's interlocutors today, to dwell at greater length on St. Matthew's words (19:3ff.). To respond to the indication, inserted in them by Christ, we will try to penetrate towards that "beginning," to which He referred in such a significant way. Thus we will follow from a distance the great work which participants in the

forthcoming Synod of Bishops are undertaking on this subject just now. Together with them, numerous groups of pastors and laymen are taking part in it, feeling particularly responsible with regard to the role which Christ assigned to marriage and the Christian family: the role that He has always given, and still gives in our age, in the modern world.

The cycle of reflections we are beginning today, with the intention of continuing it during the following Wednesday meetings has also, among other things, the purpose of accompanying, from afar, so to speak, the work of preparation for the Synod, not touching its subject directly, however, but turning our attention to the deep roots from which this subject springs.

Biblical Account
of Creation Analyzed

General audience of September 12, 1979.

1. Last Wednesday we began the series of reflections on the reply given by Christ to His questioners on the subject of the unity and indissolubility of marriage. As we recall, the Pharisees who questioned Him appealed to the Mosaic law. Christ, however, went back to the "beginning," quoting the words of the Book of Genesis.

The "beginning" in this case concerns what is treated of in one of the first pages of the Book of Genesis. If we wish to analyze this reality, we must undoubtedly direct our attention first of all to the text. In fact, the words spoken by Christ in His talk with the Pharisees—which are to be found in Matthew 19 and Mark 10—constitute a passage which in its turn is set in a well-defined context, without reference to which they can neither be understood nor correctly interpreted.

This context is provided by the words: "Have you not read that the Creator from the

beginning made them male and female...?"
(Mt. 19:4), and makes reference to the so-called
first account of the creation of man inserted in
the seven-day cycle of the creation of the world
(Gn. 1:1-2, 4). However, the context nearest to
the other words of Christ, taken from Genesis
2:24, is the so-called second account of the creation of man (Gn. 2:5-25), but indirectly it is the
entire third chapter of Genesis.

The second account of the creation of man
forms a conceptual and stylistic unity with the
description of original innocence, man's happiness, and also his first fall. Granted the
specificness of the content of Christ's words
taken from Genesis 2:24, one could also include
in the context at least the first phrase of the
fourth chapter of Genesis, which treats of the
conception and birth of man from earthly parents. And that is what we intend to do in the
present analysis.

VARIOUS ACCOUNTS
OF MAN'S CREATION

2. *From the point of view of biblical
criticism*, it is necessary to mention immediately that *the first account of man's creation is
chronologically later than the second.* The
origin of this latter is much more remote. This
more ancient text is defined as "Yahwist"
because the term "Yahweh" is used to
denominate God. It is difficult not to be struck
by the fact that the image of God presented
there has quite considerable anthropomorphic

traits (among others, we read in fact that "...the Lord God formed man of dust from the ground, and breathed into his nostrils the breath of life": Gn. 2:7).

In comparison with this description, the first account, that is, the one held to be chronologically later, is much more mature both as regards the image of God, and as regards the formulation of the essential truths about man. This account derives from the priestly and "elohist" tradition, from "Elohim," the term used in that account for God.

MALE AND FEMALE

3. Granted that in this narration man's creation as male and female—to which Jesus refers in His reply according to Matthew 19—is inserted into the seven-day cycle of the creation of the world, there could be attributed to it especially a cosmological character; man is created on earth together with the visible world. But at the same time the Creator orders him to subdue and have dominion over the earth (cf. Gn. 1:28): he is therefore placed over the world. Even though man is strictly bound to the visible world, nevertheless the biblical narrative does not speak of his likeness to the rest of creatures, but only to God ("God created man in his own image, in the image of God he created him..." Gn. 1:27). In the seven-day cycle of creation there is evident a precise graduated procedure.[1] Man, however, is not created according

to a natural succession, but the Creator seems to halt before calling him into existence, as if he were pondering within Himself to make a decision: "Let us make man in our image, after our likeness..." (Gn. 1:26).

THEOLOGICAL CHARACTER

4. The level of that first account of man's creation, even though chronologically later, is particularly of a theological character. An indication of that is especially the definition of man on the basis of his relationship with God ("in the image of God he created him"), which at the same time contains the affirmation of the absolute impossibility of reducing man to the "world." Already in the light of the first phrases of the Bible, man cannot be either understood or explained completely in terms of categories taken from the "world," that is, from the visible complex of bodies. Notwithstanding this, man also is corporeal. Genesis 1:27 observes that this essential truth about man refers both to the male and the female: "God created man in his image...male and female he created them."[2]

It must be recognized that the first account is concise, and free from any trace whatsoever of subjectivism. It contains only the objective facts and defines the objective reality, both when it speaks of man's creation, male and female, in the image of God, and when it adds a little later the words of the first blessing: "Be fruitful and multiply, and fill the earth; subdue it and have dominion over it" (Gn. 1:28).

INSPIRATION FOR THINKERS

5. The first account of man's creation, which, as we observed, is of a theological nature, conceals within itself a powerful metaphysical content. Let it not be forgotten that this very text of the Book of Genesis has become the source of the most profound inspirations for thinkers who have sought to understand "being" and "existence" (perhaps only the third chapter of Exodus can bear comparison with this text).[3] Notwithstanding certain detailed and plastic expressions of the passage, man is defined there, first of all, in the dimensions of being and of existence *("Esse")*. He is defined in a way that is more metaphysical than physical.

To this mystery of His creation ("in the image of God he created him") there corresponds the perspective of procreation ("Be fruitful and multiply, fill the earth"), of that becoming in the world and in time, of that *"fieri"* which is necessarily bound up with the metaphysical situation of creation: of contingent being *(contingens)*. Precisely in this metaphysical context of the description of Genesis 1, it is necessary to understand the entity of the good, namely, the aspect of value. Indeed, this aspect appears in the cycle of nearly all the days of creation and reaches its culmination after the creation of man: "God saw everything that he had made, and behold, it was very good" (Gn. 1:31). For this reason it can be said with certainty that the first chapter of Genesis has established an unassailable point of reference and a solid basis for a metaphysic and also for an anthropology and an ethic, according to which *"ens et bonum convertuntur"* (being and the good are convertible). Undoubtedly, all this has a significance also for theology, and especially for the theology of the body.

"THEOLOGY OF THE BODY"

6. At this point let us interrupt our considerations. In a week's time we shall deal with the second account of creation, that which, according to biblical scholars is chronologically more ancient. The expression "theology of the body" just now used deserves a more exact explanation, but we shall leave that for another occasion. First, we must seek to examine more closely that passage of the Book of Genesis to which Christ had recourse.

FOOTNOTES

1. Speaking of non-living matter, the biblical author used different predicates, like "separated," "called," "made," "placed." Speaking, however, of beings endowed with life, he uses the term "created" and "blessed." God orders them: "Be fruitful and multiply." This order refers both to animals and to man, indicating that corporality is common to both (cf. Gn. 1:22, 28).

However, man's creation is essentially distinguished, in the biblical description, from God's preceding works. Not only is it preceded by a solemn introduction, as if it were a case of God deliberating before this important act, but, above all, man's exceptional dignity is set out in relief by the "likeness" to God of whom he is the image.

Creating non-living matter, God "separated"; to the animals He gave the order to be fruitful and multiply, but the difference of sex is underlined only in regard to man ("male and female he created them") by blessing at the same time their fruitfulness, that is, the bond of the persons (Gn. 1:27, 28).

2. The original text states: "God created man *(ha-adam*—a collective noun: 'humanity'?), in his own image; in the image of God he created him; male *(zakar*—masculine) and female *(uneqebah*—feminine) he created them" (Gn. 1:27).

3. *"Haec sublimis veritas"*: "I am who I am" (Ex. 3:14) constitutes an object of reflection for many philosophers, beginning from St. Augustine who held that Plato must have known this text because it seemed very close to his ideas. The Augustinian doctrine of the divine *"essentialitas"* has exercised, through St. Anselm, a profound influence on the theology of Richard of St. Victor, of Alexander of Hales and of St. Bonaventure.

"To pass from this philosophical interpretation of Exodus to that put forward by St. Thomas, one had necessarily to bridge the gap that separated 'the being of essence' from 'the being of existence.' The Thomistic proofs of the existence of God bridged it."

Different from this is the position of Master Eckhart, who on the basis of this text attributes to God the *"puritas essendi"*: *"est aliquid altius ente..."* ("the purity of being: He is something higher than *ens"*) (cf. E. Gilson, *Le Thomisme*, Paris 1944 [Vrin] pp. 122-127. E. Gilson, *History of Christian Philosophy in the Middle Ages*, London 1955 [Sheed and Ward] 810).

The Second Account
of Creation:
The Subjective Definition
of Man

General audience of September 19, 1979.

1. With reference to Christ's words on the subject of marriage, in which He appeals to the "beginning," we directed our attention last week to the first account of man's creation in the Book of Genesis (chap. 1). Today we shall pass to the second account which is frequently described as the "Yahwist," since God is called by the name of "Yahweh" in it.

The second account of man's creation (linked to the presentation both of original innocence and happiness and of the first fall) has by its nature a different character. While not wishing to anticipate the particulars of this narrative—because it will be better for us to recall them in later analyses—we should note that the entire text, in formulating the truth about man, amazes us with its typical profundity, different from that of the first chapter of Genesis.

ANCIENT DESCRIPTION

It can be said that it is a profundity that is of a nature particularly subjective, and therefore, in a certain sense, psychological. The second chapter of Genesis constitutes, in a certain manner, the most ancient description and record of man's self-knowledge, and together with the third chapter it is the first testimony of human conscience. A reflection in depth on this text—through the whole archaic form of the narrative, which manifests its primitive mythical character[1]—provides us "in nucleo" with nearly all the elements of the analysis of man, to which modern, and especially contemporary philosophical anthropology is sensitive. It could be said that Genesis 2 presents the creation of man especially in its subjective aspect. Comparing both accounts, we arrive at the conclusion that this subjectivity corresponds to the objective reality of man created "in the image of God." This fact, also, is—in another way—important for the theology of the body, as we shall see in subsequent analyses.

FIRST HUMAN BEING

2. It is significant that Christ, in His reply to the Pharisees, in which He appealed to the "beginning," indicates first of all the creation of man by referring to Genesis 1:27: "The Creator from the beginning created them male and female"; only afterwards does He quote the text of Genesis 2:24. The words which directly de-

scribe the unity and indissolubility of marriage are found in the immediate context of the second account of creation, whose characteristic feature is the separate creation of woman (cf. Gn. 2:18-23), while the account of the creation of the first man is found in Genesis 2:5-7.

The first human being the Bible calls "Man" *('adam)*, but from the moment of the creation of the first woman, it begins to call him "man," *(ish)*, in relation to *ishshah* ("woman," because she was taken from the man = *ish*).[2]

It is also significant that Christ, in referring to Genesis 2:24, not only links the "beginning" with the mystery of creation, but also leads us, one might say, to the limit of man's primitive innocence and of original sin. The second description of man's creation is placed by the Book of Genesis precisely in this context. There we read first of all: "And the rib which the Lord God had taken from the man he made into a woman and brought her to the man; then the man said: 'This at last is bone of my bones and flesh of my flesh; she shall be called Woman, because she was taken out of Man'" (Gn. 2:22-23). "Therefore a man leaves his father and his mother and cleaves to his wife, and they become one flesh" (Gn. 2:24). "And the man and his wife were both naked, and they were not ashamed" (Gn. 2:25).

TREE OF KNOWLEDGE

3. Immediately after these verses, chapter 3 begins with its account of the first fall of

the man and the woman, linked with the mysterious tree already called the "tree of the knowledge of good and evil" (Gn. 2:17). Thus there emerges an entirely new situation, essentially different from the preceding. The tree of knowledge of good and evil is the line of demarcation between the two original situations of which the Book of Genesis speaks.

The first situation was that of original innocence, in which man (male and female) is, as it were, outside the sphere of the knowledge of good and evil, until the moment when he transgresses the Creator's prohibition and eats the fruit of the tree of knowledge. The second situation, however, is that in which man, after having disobeyed the Creator's command at the prompting of the evil spirit, symbolized by the serpent, finds himself, in a certain way, within the sphere of the knowledge of good and evil. This second situation determines the state of human sinfulness, in contrast to the state of primitive innocence.

Even though the "Yahwist" text is, all for all, very concise, nevertheless it suffices to differentiate and to set against each other with clarity those two original situations. We speak here of situations, having before our eyes the account which is a description of events. Nonetheless, by means of this description and all its particulars, there emerges the essential difference between the state of man's sinfulness and that of his original innocence.[3]

Systematic theology will discern in these two antithetical situations two different states of human nature: the state of integral nature and the state of fallen nature. All this emerges from that "Yahwist" text of Genesis 2 and 3, which contains in itself the most ancient word of revelation, and evidently has a fundamental significance for the theology of man and for the theology of the body.

THE "YAHWIST" TEXT

4. When Christ, referring to the "beginning," directs His questioners to the words written in Genesis 2:24, He orders them, in a certain sense, to go beyond the boundary which, in the "Yahwist" text of Genesis, runs between the first and second situation of man. He does not approve what Moses had permitted "for their hardness of heart," and He appeals to the words of the first divine regulation, which in this text is expressly linked to man's state of original innocence. This means that this regulation has not lost its force, even though man has lost his primitive innocence.

Christ's reply is decisive and unequivocal. Therefore, we must draw from it the normative conclusions which have an essential significance not only for ethics, but especially for the theology of man and for the theology of the body, which as a particular element of theological anthropology is constituted on the basis of the Word of God which is revealed. During the next meeting we shall seek to draw these conclusions.

FOOTNOTES

1. If in the language of the rationalism of the 19th century, the term "myth" indicated what was not contained in reality, the product of the imagination (Wundt), or what is irrational (Levy-Bruhl), the 20th century has modified the concept of myth.

L. Walk sees in myth natural philosophy, primitive and areligious: R. Otto considers it as the instrument of religious knowledge: for C.G. Jung, however, myth is the manifestation of the archetypes and the expression of the "collective unconsciousness," the symbol of the interior processes.

M. Eliade discovers in myth the structure of the reality that is inaccessible to rational and empirical investigation. Myth, in fact, transforms the event into a category, and makes us capable of perceiving the transcendental reality. It is not merely a symbol of the interior processes (as Jung states), but it is an autonomous and creative act of the human spirit, by means of which revelation is realized (cf. *Traité d'histoire des religions*, Paris 1949, p. 363; *Images et symboles*, Paris 1952, pp. 199-235).

According to P. Tillich myth is a symbol, constituted by the elements of reality to present the absolute and the transcendence of being, to which the religious act tends.

H. Schlier emphasizes that the myth does not know historical facts and has no need of them, inasmuch as it describes man's cosmic destiny which is always identical.

In short, the myth tends to know what is unknowable.

According to P. Ricoeur: "The myth is something other than an explanation of the world, of its history and its destiny. It expresses in terms of the world, indeed of what is beyond the world, or of a second world, the understanding that man has of himself through relation with the fundamental and the limit of his existence.... It expresses in an objective language the understanding that man has of his dependence in regard to what lies at the limit and the origin of his world" (P. Ricoeur, *Le conflit des interprétations*, Paris [Seuil] 1969, p. 383).

"The Adamic myth is *par excellence* the anthropological myth. Adam means Man: but not every myth of the 'primordial man' is an 'Adamic myth' which...alone is truly anthropological. By this three features are denoted:

"—the aetiological myth relates the origin of evil to an *ancestor* of present mankind, whose condition is homogeneous with ours....

"'—the aetiological myth is the most extreme attempt to separate the origin of evil from that of good. The aim of this myth is to establish firmly that evil has a radical origin, distinct from the more primitive source of the goodness of things.... This distinction of what is radical and what is primitive is essential to the anthropological character of the Adamic myth. It is that which traces back to man the origin of evil placed in a creation which owes its absolute beginning to a creative act of God.

"'—the Adamic myth subordinates to the central figure of primordial man other figures which tend to displace the center of the narrative, without, however, suppressing the primacy of the Adamic figure....

"The myth, in naming Adam, man, makes explicit the concrete universality of human evil; the spirit of penitence is given in the Adamic myth the symbol of this universality. Thus we find again...the universalizing function of the myth. But at the same time, we find the two other functions, equally called forth by the penitential experience.... The proto-historical myth thus serves not only to make general to mankind of all times and of all places the experience of Israel, but to extend to mankind the great tension of the condemnation and of mercy which the prophets had taught Israel to discern in its own destiny.

"Finally, the last function of the myth, which finds a motive in the faith of Israel: *the myth prepares for speculation* in exploring the point where the ontological and the historical part company" (P. Ricoeur, *Finitude et culpabilité: II Symbolique du mal*, Paris 1960 [Aubier], pp. 218-227).

2. As regards etymology, it is not excluded that the Hebrew term *ish* is derived from a root which signifies "strength" (*ish* or *wsh:*) whereas *ishshah* is linked to a series of Semitic terms whose meaning varies between "woman" and "wife."

The etymology proposed by the biblical text is of a popular character and serves to underline the unity of the origin of man and woman. This seems to be confirmed by the assonance of both terms.

3. "Religious language itself calls for the transposition from 'images' or rather 'symbolic modalities' to 'conceptual modalities' of expression.

"At first sight this transposition might appear to be a purely *extrinsic change*. Symbolic language seems inadequate to introduce the concept because of a reason that is peculiar to Western culture. In this culture religious language has always been conditioned by another language, the philosophical, which is the conceptual language *par excellence*.... If it is true that a religious vocabulary is understood only in a community which interprets it and according to a tradition of interpretation, it is also true that there does not exist a tradition of interpretation that is not 'mediated' by some philosophical conception.

"So the word 'God,' which in the biblical texts receives its meaning from the *convergence* of different modes of discourse (narratives, prophecies, legislative texts and wisdom literature, proverbs and hymns)—viewing this convergence both as the point of intersection and as the horizon evasive of any and every form—had to be absorbed in the conceptual space, in order to be reinterpreted in terms of the philosophical Absolute, as the first Mover, first Cause, *Actus Essendi*, perfect Being, etc. Our concept of God pertains, therefore, to an onto-theology, in which there is organized the entire constellation of the key-words of theological semantics, but in a framework of meanings dictated by metaphysics" (Paul Ricoeur, *Ermeneutica biblica*, Brescia 1978, Morcelliana, pp. 140-141; original title. *Biblical Hermeneutics*, Montana 1975).

The question, whether the metaphysical reduction really expresses the content which the symbolical and metaphorical language conceals within itself, is another matter.

Boundary Between Original Innocence and Redemption

General audience of September 26, 1979.

1. Christ, answering the question on the unity and indissolubility of marriage, referred to what was written on the subject of marriage in the Book of Genesis. In our two preceding reflections we analyzed both the so-called "Elohist" text (Gn. 1) and the "Yahwist" one (Gn. 2). Today we wish to draw some conclusions from these analyses.

When Christ refers to the "beginning," He asks His questioners to go beyond, in a certain sense, the boundary which, in the Book of Genesis, passes between the state of original innocence and that of sinfulness, which started with the original fall.

Symbolically this boundary can be linked with the tree of the knowledge of good and evil, which in the Yahwist text delimits two diametrically opposed situations: the situation of original innocence and that of original sin. These situations have a specific dimension in man, in his inner self, in his knowledge, conscience, choice and decision, and all that in relation to God the Creator who, in the Yahwist text (Gn. 2 and 3) is, at the same time, the God of the Covenant, of the most ancient covenant of the Creator with His creature, that is, with man.

The tree of the knowledge of good and evil, as expression and symbol of the covenant with God broken in man's heart, delimits and contrasts two diametrically opposed situations and states: that of original innocence and that of original sin, and at the same time of man's hereditary sinfulness which is derived from it. However, *Christ's words,* which refer to the "beginning," *enable us to find in man an essential continuity and a link* between these two different states or dimensions of the human being.

The state of sin is part of "historical man," both of the one of whom we read in Matthew 19, that is Christ's questioner at that time, and also of any other potential or actual questioner of all times of history, and therefore, naturally, also of modern man. That state, however—the "historical" state—plunges its roots, in every man without any exception, in his own theological "prehistory," which is the state of original innocence.

FUNDAMENTAL INNOCENCE

2. It is not a question here of mere dialectic. The laws of knowing correspond to those of

being. It is impossible to understand the state of "historical" sinfulness, without referring or appealing (and Christ, in fact, appeals to it) to the state of original (in a certain sense, "prehistoric") and fundamental innocence. Therefore, the arising of sinfulness as a state, a dimension of human existence is, right from the beginning, in relation to this real innocence of man as his original and fundamental state, as a dimension of the being created "in the image of God."

It happens in this way not only for the first man, male and female, as *dramatis personae* and leading characters of the events described in the Yahwist text of chapters 2 and 3 of Genesis, but also for the whole historical course of human existence. *Historical man is therefore, so to speak, rooted in his revealed theological prehistory;* and so every point of his historical sinfulness is explained (both for the soul and for the body) with reference to original innocence. It can be said that this reference is a "coinheritance" of sin, and precisely of original sin. If this sin signifies, in every historical man, a state of lost grace, then it also contains a reference to that grace, which was precisely the grace of original innocence.

ST. PAUL'S REFERENCE

3. When Christ, according to chapter 19 of Matthew, makes reference to the "beginning," by this expression He does not indicate merely the state of original innocence as the lost hori-

zon of human existence in history. To the words which He utters with His own lips, we have the right to attribute at the same time the whole eloquence of the mystery of redemption. In fact, already in the Yahwist texts of Genesis 2 and 3, we are witnesses of when man, male and female, after breaking the original covenant with his Creator, receives the first promise of redemption in the words of the so-called Proto-gospel in Genesis 3:15,[1] and begins to live *in the theological perspective of the redemption.*

In the same way, therefore, "historical" man—both Christ's questioner at that time, of whom Matthew 19 speaks, and modern man—participates in this perspective. He participates not only in the history of human sinfulness, as a hereditary and at the same time personal and unique subject of this history, but he also participates in the history of salvation, here, too, as its subject and co-creator. He is, therefore, not only closed, because of his sinfulness, with regard to original innocence—but is at the same time open to the mystery of redemption, which was accomplished in Christ and through Christ.

THEOLOGICAL PERSPECTIVE

Paul, the author of the Letter to the Romans, expresses this perspective of redemption in which "historical" man lives, when he writes: "...we ourselves, who have the first fruits of the Spirit, groan inwardly as we wait for...the redemption of our bodies" (Rom. 8:23). We cannot lose sight of this perspective as we follow the words of Christ who, in His talk on the indissolubility of marriage, appeals to the "beginning."

If that "beginning" indicated only the creation of man as "male and female," if—as we have already mentioned—it brought the questioners only over the boundary of man's state of sin to original innocence, and did not open at the same time the perspective of a "redemption of the body," Christ's answer would not at all be understood adequately. It is precisely this perspective of the redemption of the body that guarantees the continuity and unity between the hereditary state of man's sin and his original innocence, although this innocence was, historically, lost by him irremediably. It is clear, too, that Christ has every right to answer the question posed by the doctors of the law and of the covenant (as we read in Matthew 19 and in Mark 10), in the perspective of the redemption on which the covenant itself rests.

METHOD OF ANALYSES

4. If, in the context of the theology of corporeal man, substantially outlined in this way, we think of the method of further analyses about the revelation of the "beginning," in which reference to the first chapters of the Book of Genesis is essential, we must at once turn our attention to a factor which is particularly important for the theological interpretation: important because it consists in the relationship between revelation and experience.

In the interpretation of the revelation about man, and especially about the body, we must, for understandable reasons, refer to experience, since corporeal man is perceived by us mainly by experience. In the light of the above-mentioned fundamental considerations, we have every right to the conviction that this "historical" experience of ours must, in a certain way, stop at the threshold of man's original innocence, since it is inadequate in relation to it. However, in the light of the same introductory considerations, we must arrive at the conviction that our human experience is, in this case, to some extent a legitimate means for the theological interpretation, and is, in a certain sense, an indispensable point of reference, which we must keep in mind in the interpretation of the "beginning." A more detailed analysis of the text will enable us to have a clearer view of it.

SUBSEQUENT ANALYSES

5. It seems that the words of the Letter to the Romans 8:23, just quoted, render in the best way the direction of our researches centered on the revelation of that "beginning" to which Christ referred in His talk on the indissolubility of marriage (Mt. 19 and Mk. 10). All the subsequent analyses that will be made on the basis of the first chapters of Genesis will almost necessarily reflect the truth of Paul's words: "We who have the first fruit of the Spirit groan inwardly as we wait for...the redemption

of our bodies." If we put ourselves in this position—so deeply in agreement with experience[2]
—the "beginning" must speak to us with the
great richness of light that comes from revelation, to which above all theology wishes to be
accountable. The continuation of the analyses
will explain to us why and in what sense this
must be a theology of the body.

FOOTNOTES

1. Already the Greek translation of the Old Testament,
the Septuagint, which goes back to about the 2nd century
B.C., interprets Genesis 3:15 in the Messianic sense, applying the masculine pronoun *autós* in reference to the Greek
neuter noun *sperma* (*semen* in the Vulgate). The Judaic
tradition continues this interpretation.

Christian exegesis, beginning with St. Irenaeus (*Adv.
Haer.* III, 23, 7), sees this text as "protogospel," which
announces the victory won by Jesus Christ over Satan.
Although in the last few centuries scripture scholars have
interpreted this pericope differently, and some of them
challenge the Messianic interpretation, in recent times,
however, there has been a return to it under a rather different aspect. The Yahwist author unites prehistory, in fact,
with the history of Israel, which reaches its peak in the Messianic dynasty of David, which will fulfill the promises of
Genesis 3:15 (cf. 2 Sam. 7:12).

The New Testament illustrated the fulfillment of the
promise in the same Messianic perspective: Jesus is the
Messiah, descendant of David (Rom. 1:3; 2 Tim. 2:8), born
of woman (Gal. 4:4), a new Adam-David (1 Cor. 15), who
must reign "until he has put all his enemies under his feet"
(1 Cor. 15:25). Finally Revelation 12:1-10 presents the final
fulfillment of the prophecy of Genesis 3:15, which while not
being a clear and direct announcement of Jesus as Messiah
of Israel, leads to Him, however, through the royal and Messianic tradition that unites the Old and the New Testament.

2. Speaking here of the relationship between "experience" and "revelation," indeed of a surprising convergence between them, we wish merely to say that man, in
his present state of existing in the body, experiences

numerous limitations, sufferings, passions, weaknesses and finally death itself, which, at the same time, refer this existence of his in the body to another and different state or dimension. When St. Paul writes of the "redemption of the body," he speaks with the language of revelation; experience, in fact, is not able to grasp this content or rather this reality. At the same time, in this content as a whole, the author of Romans 8:23 includes everything that is offered both to him and, in a certain way, to every man (independently of his relationship with revelation) through the experience of human existence, which is an existence in the body.

We have, therefore, the right to speak of the relationship between experience and revelation; in fact, we have the right to raise the problem of their mutual relation, even if, for many people, there passes between them a line of demarcation which is a line of complete antithesis and radical antinomy. This line, in their opinion, must certainly be drawn between faith and science, between theology and philosophy. In the formulation of this point of view, abstract considerations rather than man as a living subject are taken into consideration.

Meaning of Man's Original Solitude

General audience of October 10, 1979.

1. In the last reflection of the present cycle we reached an introductory conclusion, taken from the words of the Book of Genesis on the creation of man as male and female. We reached these words, that is, the "beginning," to which the Lord Jesus referred in His talk on the indissolubility of marriage (cf. Mt. 19:3-9; Mk. 10:1-12). But the conclusion at which we arrived does not yet end the series of our analyses. We must, in fact, reread the narrations of the first and second chapters of the Book of Genesis in a wider context, which will allow us to establish a series of meanings of the ancient text to which Christ referred. Today, therefore, we will reflect on the meaning of man's original solitude.

SOLITUDE OF "MAN" AS SUCH

2. The starting point of this reflection is provided for us directly by the following words of the Book of Genesis: "It is not good that man (male) should be alone; I will make him a helper fit for him" (Gn. 2:18). It is God-Yahweh who

speaks these words. They belong to the second account of the creation of man, and so they come from the Yahwist tradition. As we already recalled before, it is significant that, as regards the Yahwist text, the account of the creation of man (male) is a separate passage (Gn. 2:7), which precedes the account of the creation of the first woman (Gn. 2:21-22). It is also significant that the first man *('adam)*, created from "dust from the ground," is defined as a "male" *('is)* only after the creation of the first woman. And so when God-Yahweh speaks the words about solitude, it is in reference to the solitude of "man" as such, and not just to that of the male.[1]

It is difficult, however, merely on the basis of this fact, to go very far in drawing conclusions. Nevertheless, the complete context of that solitude of which Genesis 2:18 speaks can convince us that it is a question here of the solitude of "man" (male and female) and not just of the solitude of man the male, caused by the lack of woman. It seems, therefore, on the basis of the whole context, that this solitude has two meanings: one derived from man's very nature, that is, from his humanity (and that is evident in the account of Genesis 2), and the other derived from the male-female relationship, and that is evident, in a certain way, on the basis of the first meaning. A detailed analysis of the description seems to confirm this.

3. The problem of solitude is manifested only in the context of the second account of the

creation of man. The first account ignores this problem. There man is created in one act as "male and female" ("God created man in his own image...male and female he created them" Gn. 1:27). The second account which, as we have already mentioned, speaks first of the creation of the man and only afterwards of the creation of the woman from the "rib" of the male, concentrates our attention on the fact that "man is alone"; and that appears a fundamental anthropological problem, prior, in a certain sense, to the one raised by the fact that this man is male and female. This problem is prior not so much in the chronological sense, as in the existential sense: it is prior "by its very nature." The problem of man's solitude from the point of view of the theology of the body will also be revealed as such, if we succeed in making a thorough analysis of the second account of creation in Genesis 2.

A SPECIFIC TEST

4. The affirmation of God-Yahweh, "It is not good that man should be alone," appears not only in the immediate context of the decision to create woman ("I will make him a helper fit for him"), but also in the wider context of reasons and circumstances, which explain more deeply the meaning of man's original solitude. The Yahwist text connects the creation of man first and foremost with the need to "till the ground" (Gn. 2:5), and that would correspond, in the first account, with the vocation

to subdue and have dominion over the earth (cf. Gn. 1:28). Then, the second account of creation speaks of man being put in the "garden in Eden," and in this way introduces us to the state of his original happiness. Up to this moment man is the object of the creative action of God-Yahweh, who at the same time, as legislator, establishes the conditions of the first covenant with man.

Man's subjectivity is already emphasized through this. It finds a further expression when the Lord God "formed out of the ground every beast of the field and every bird of the air, and brought them to man to see what he would call them" (Gn. 2:19). In this way, therefore, the first meaning of man's original solitude is defined on the basis of a specific test, or examination, which man undergoes before God (and in a certain way also before himself). By means of this test, man becomes aware of his own superiority, that is, that he cannot be considered on the same footing as any other species of living beings on the earth.

In fact, as the text says, "whatever the man called every living creature, that was its name" (Gn. 2:19). "The man gave names to all cattle, and to the birds of the air, and to every beast of the field; but for the man (male) there was not found a helper fit for him" (Gn. 2:20).

CREATION OF WOMAN

5. All this part of the text is unquestionably a preparation for the account of the

creation of woman. However, it possesses a
deep meaning even apart from this creation.
For created man finds himself, right from the
first moment of his existence, before God as if in
search of his own entity; it could be said: in
search of the definition of himself. A contemporary would say: in search of his own
"identity." The fact that man "is alone" in the
midst of the visible world and, in particular,
among living beings, has a negative significance in this search, since it expresses what he
"is not." Nevertheless, the fact of not being able
to identify himself essentially with the visible
world of other living beings *(animalia)* has, at
the same time, a positive aspect for this primary
search. Even if this fact is not yet a complete
definition, it constitutes, however, one of its
elements. If we accept the Aristotelian tradition
in logic and in anthropology, it would be
necessary to define this element as the "proximate genus" *(genus proximum)*.[2]

6. The Yahwist text enables us, however,
to discover also further elements in that
admirable passage, in which man finds himself
alone before God mainly to express, through a
first self-definition, his own self-knowledge, as
the original and fundamental manifestation of
mankind. Self-knowledge develops at the same
rate as knowledge of the world, of all the visible
creatures, of all the living beings to which man
has given a name to affirm his own dissimilarity
with regard to them. In this way, therefore, consciousness reveals man as the one who posses-

ses the cognitive faculty as regards the visible world. With this knowledge which, in a certain way, brings him out of his own being, man at the same time reveals himself to himself in all the peculiarity of his being. He is not only essentially and subjectively alone. Solitude, in fact, also signifies man's subjectivity, which is constituted through self-knowledge. Man is alone because he is "different" from the visible world, from the world of living beings. Analyzing the text of the Book of Genesis we are, in a way, witnesses of how man "distinguishes himself" before God-Yahweh from the whole world of living beings (animalia) with his first act of self-consciousness, and of how, therefore, he reveals himself to himself and at the same time asserts himself as a "person" in the visible world. That process sketched so incisively in Genesis 2:19-20, a process of search for a definition of himself, leads not only to indicating—linking up with the Aristotelian tradition—the *proximate genus*, which in chapter 2 of Genesis is expressed with the words: "the man gave names," to which there corresponds the *specific differentia* which is, according to Aristotle's definition, *nôus, zōón noētikón*. This process also leads to the *first delineation* of the human being as a human *person* with the specific subjectivity that characterizes him.

FOOTNOTES

1. The Hebrew text constantly calls the first man *ha-'adam*, while the term *'is* ("male") is introduced only when contrasted with *'issa* ("female").

So "man" was solitary without reference to sex.

In the translation into some European languages it is difficult, however, to express this concept of Genesis, because "man" and "male" are usually defined with one word: "homo," "uomo," "homme," "man."

2. "An essential (quidditive) definition is a statement which explains the essence or nature of things.

It will be essential when we can define a thing by its *proximate genus* and *specific differentia*.

The *proximate genus* includes within its comprehension all the essential elements of the genera above it and, therefore, includes all the beings that are cognate or similar in nature to the thing that is being defined; the *specific differentia*, on the other hand, brings in the distinctive element which separates this thing from all others of a similar nature, by showing in what manner it is different from all others, with which it might be erroneously identified.

"Man" is defined as a "rational animal"; "animal" is his proximate genus, "rational" is his specific differentia. The proximate genus "animal" includes within its comprehension all the essential elements of the genera above it, because an animal is a "sentient, living, material substance" (...). The specific differentia "rational" is the one distinctive essential element which distinguishes "man" from every other "animal." It therefore makes him a species of his own and separates him from every other "animal" and every other genus above animal, including plants, inanimate bodies and substance.

Furthermore, since the specific differentia is the distinctive element in the essence of man, it includes all the characteristic "properties" which lie in the nature of man as man, namely, power of speech, morality, etc., realities which are absent in all other beings in this physical world."

(C.N. Bittle, *The Science of Correct Thinking, Logic,* Milwaukee 1947[12], pp. 73-74).

Man's Awareness
of Being a Person

General audience of October 24, 1979.

1. At the preceding talk we began to analyze the meaning of man's original solitude. The starting point was given to us by the Yahwist text, and in particular by the following words: "It is not good that the man should be alone: I will make him a helper fit for him" (Gn. 2:18). The analysis of the relative passages in the Book of Genesis (chap. 2) has already brought us to surprising conclusions which concern the anthropology, that is, the fundamental science about man, contained in this Book. In fact, in relatively few sentences, the ancient text portrays man as a person with the subjectivity that characterizes him.

When God-Yahweh gives this first man, so formed, the order that concerns all the trees that grow in the "garden in Eden," particularly the tree of the knowledge of good and evil, there is added to the features of the man, described above, the moment of choice and self-determination, that is, of free will. In this way, the image of man, as a person endowed with a subjectivity of his own, appears before us, as it were, completed in his first outline.

In the concept of original solitude are included both self-consciousness and self-determination. The fact that man is "alone" conceals within it this ontological structure and is at the same time an indication of true comprehension. Without that, we cannot understand correctly the subsequent words, which constitute the prelude to the creation of the first woman: "I will make a helper." But above all, without that deep significance of man's original solitude, it is not possible to understand and interpret correctly the whole situation of man, created "in the image of God," which is the situation of the first, or rather original, covenant with God.

PARTNER OF THE ABSOLUTE

2. This man, about whom the narrative in the first chapter says that he was created "in the image of God," is manifested in the second narrative as subject of the covenant, that is, a subject constituted as a person, constituted in the dimension of "partner of the Absolute" since he must consciously discern and choose between good and evil, between life and death. The words of the first order of God-Yahweh (Gn. 2:16-17), which speak directly of the submission and dependence of man the creature on his Creator, indirectly reveal precisely this level of humanity as subject of the covenant and "partner of the Absolute." Man is "alone": that

means that he, through his own humanity, through what he is, is constituted at the same time in a unique, exclusive and unrepeatable relationship with God Himself. The anthropological definition contained in the Yahwist text approaches, on its part, what is expressed in the theological definition of man, which we find in the first narrative of creation ("Let us make man in our image, after our likeness": Gn. 1:26).

CONSCIOUS OF BEING "ALONE"

3. Man, thus formed, belongs to the visible world; he is a body among bodies. Taking up again and, in a way, reconstructing the meaning of original solitude, we apply it to man in his totality. His body, through which man participates in the visible created world, makes him at the same time conscious of being "alone." Otherwise, he would not have been able to arrive at that conviction which, in fact, as we read, he reached (cf. Gn. 2:20), if his body had not helped him to understand it, making the matter evident. Consciousness of solitude might have been shattered precisely because of his body itself. The man, 'adam, might have reached the conclusion, on the basis of the experience of his own body, that he was substantially similar to other living beings (animalia). But, on the contrary, as we read, he did not arrive at this conclusion; in fact, he reached the conviction that he was "alone." The Yahwist text never speaks directly of the body; even

when it says that "the Lord God formed man of dust from the ground," it speaks of man and not of his body. Nevertheless, the narrative taken as a whole offers us a sufficient basis to perceive this man, created in the visible world, precisely as a body among bodies.

The analysis of the Yahwist text also enables us to *link man's original solitude with consciousness of the body,* through which man is distinguished from all the *animalia* and "is separated" from them, and also *through which* he is *a person.* It can be affirmed with certainty that that man, thus formed, has at the same time consciousness and awareness of the meaning of his own body. And that on the basis of the experience of original solitude.

MEANING OF HIS CORPORALITY

4. All that can be considered as an implication of the second narrative of the creation of man, and the analysis of the text enables us to develop it amply.

When at the beginning of the Yahwist text, even before it speaks of the creation of man from "dust of the ground," we read that "there was no one to till the land or to make channels of water spring out of the earth to irrigate the whole land" (Gn. 2:5-6), we rightly associate this passage with the one in the first narrative, in which God's command is expressed: "Fill the earth and subdue it; and have dominion..." (Gn. 1:28). The second narrative alludes specifically to the work that man carries out to till the earth.

The first fundamental means to dominate the earth lies in man himself. Man can dominate the earth because he alone—and no other of the living beings—is capable of "tilling it" and transforming it according to his own needs ("he made channels of water spring out of the earth to irrigate the whole land"). And lo, this first outline of a specifically human activity seems to belong to the definition of man, as it emerges from the analysis of the Yahwist text. Consequently, it can be affirmed that this outline is intrinsic to the meaning of the original solitude and belongs to that dimension of solitude through which man, from the beginning, is in the visible world as a body among bodies and discovers the meaning of his own corporality.

In the Very Definition of Man the Alternative Between Death and Immortality

General audience of October 31, 1979.

MAN, A LIVING BEING

1. Today it is opportune to return once more to the meaning of man's original solitude, which emerges above all from the analysis of the so-called Yahwist text of Genesis 2. The biblical text enables us, as we have already seen in preceding reflections, to stress not only consciousness of the human body (man is created in the visible world as a "body among bodies"), but also that of its meaning.

In view of the great conciseness of the biblical text, it is admittedly not possible to amplify this implication too much. It is certain, however, that here we touch upon the central problem of anthropology. Consciousness of the body seems to be identified in this case with the discovery of the complexity of one's own structure which, on the basis of philosophical anthropology, consists, in short, in the relationship between soul and body. The Yahwist narrative with its own language (that is, with its own terminology), expresses it by saying: "The Lord God formed man of dust from the ground, and breathed into his nostrils the breath of life; and man became a living being" (Gn. 2:7).[1] And precisely this man, "a living being," distinguishes himself continually from all other living beings in the visible world.

The premise of man's distinguishing himself in this way is precisely the fact that only he is capable of "tilling the earth" (cf. Gn. 2:5) and "subduing it" (cf. Gn. 1:28). It can be said that the consciousness of "superiority," contained in the definition of humanity, is born right from the beginning on the basis of a typically human praxis or behavior. This consciousness brings with it a particular perception of the meaning of one's own body, emerging precisely from the fact that it falls to man to "till the earth" and "subdue it." All that would be impossible without a typically human intuition of the meaning of one's own body.

EXPRESSES THE PERSON

2. It seems necessary, then, to speak in the first place of this aspect, rather than of the problem of anthropological complexity in the metaphysical sense. If the original description of human consciousness, given by the Yahwist text, comprises, in the narrative as a whole, also the body; if it contains, as it were, the first testimony of the discovery of one's corporality

(and even, as has been said, the perception of the meaning of one's own body), all that is revealed not on the basis of any primordial metaphysical analysis, but on the basis of a concrete subjectivity of man that is quite clear.

Man is a subject not only because of his self-awareness and self-determination, but also on the basis of his own body. The structure of this body is such as to permit him to be the author of a truly human activity. In this activity the body expresses the person. It is, therefore, in all its materiality ("God formed man of dust from the ground"), almost penetrable and transparent, in such a way as to make it clear who man is (and who he should be) thanks to the structure of his consciousness and of his self-determination. On this there rests the fundamental perception of the meaning of one's own body, which cannot but be discovered when analyzing man's original solitude.

EXPERIENCE OF EXISTING

3. And here, with this fundamental understanding of the meaning of his own body, man, as subject of the ancient covenant with the Creator, is placed before the mystery of the tree of knowledge. "You may freely eat of every tree of the garden; but of the tree of the knowledge of good and evil you shall not eat, for in the day that you eat of it you shall die" (Gn. 2:16-17). The original meaning of man's solitude is based on experience of the existence obtained from

the Creator. This human existence is characterized precisely by subjectivity, which includes also the meaning of the body.

But could man, who, in his original consciousness, knows exclusively the experience of existing and therefore of life, could man have understood the meaning of the words "you shall die"? Would he have been able to *arrive at understanding* the meaning of these words through the complex structure of life, given to him when "the Lord God...breathed into his nostrils the breath of life..."? It must be admitted that the word "die," a completely new one, appeared on the horizon of man's consciousness without his having ever experienced its reality, and that at the same time this word appeared before him as a radical antithesis of all that man had been endowed with.

Man heard for the first time the words "you shall die," without having any familiarity with them in his experience up to then. But on the other hand, he could not but associate the meaning of death with that dimension of life which he had enjoyed up to then. The words of God-Yahweh addressed to man confirmed a dependence in existing, such as to make man a limited being and, by his very nature, liable to nonexistence.

These words raised the problem of death in a conditional way: "in the day that you eat of it you shall die." Man, who had heard these words, had to find their truth in the very interior structure of his own solitude. And, in short, it depended on him, on his decision and free choice, if, with solitude, he was to enter also the circle of the antithesis revealed to him by the Creator, together with the tree of the knowledge of good and evil, and thereby to make his own the experience of dying and death.

Listening to the words of God-Yahweh, man should have understood that the tree of knowledge had roots not only in the "garden in Eden," but also in his humanity. He should have understood, furthermore, that that mysterious tree concealed within it a dimension of loneliness, hitherto unknown, with which the Creator had endowed him in the midst of the world of living beings, to which he, man—in the presence of the Creator Himself—had "given names," in order to arrive at the understanding that none of them was similar to him.

CREATED FROM DUST

4. When, therefore, the fundamental meaning of his body had already been established through the distinction from all other creatures, when it had thereby become clear that the "invisible" determines man more than the "visible," then there was presented to him the alternative closely and directly connected by God with the tree of the knowledge of good and evil. *The alternative between death and immortality,* which emerges from Genesis 2:17, goes beyond the essential meaning of man's body, since it grasps the eschatological meaning not only of the body, but of humanity

itself, distinguished from all living beings, from "bodies." This alternative concerns, however, in a quite particular way, the body created from "dust from the ground."

In order not to prolong this analysis any longer, we will merely note that the alternative between death and immortality enters, right from the outset, the definition of man and belongs "from the beginning" to the meaning of his solitude before God Himself. This original meaning of solitude, permeated by the alternative between death and immortality, has also a fundamental meaning for the whole theology of the body.

With this observation we conclude for the present our reflections on the meaning of man's original solitude. This observation, which emerges in a clear and penetrating way from the texts of the Book of Genesis, induces reflection both on the texts and on man, who is, perhaps, too little conscious of the truth that concerns him, and which is already contained in the first chapters of the Bible.

FOOTNOTE

1.   Biblical anthropology distinguishes in man not so much "the body" and "the soul" as "body" and "life."
   The biblical author presents here the conferring of the gift of life through "breath," which does not cease to belong to God: when God takes it away, man returns to dust, from which he was made (cf. Job 34:14-15; Ps. 104:29f.).

Original Unity
of Man and Woman

General audience of November 7, 1979.

1. The words of the Book of Genesis, "It is not good that the man should be alone" (2:18), are, as it were, a prelude to the narrative of the creation of woman. Together with this narrative, the sense of original solitude becomes part of the meaning of original unity, the key point of which seems to be precisely the words of Genesis 2:24, to which Christ refers in His talk with the Pharisees: "A man shall leave his father and mother and be joined to his wife, and the two shall become one flesh" (Mt. 19:5). If Christ, referring to the "beginning," quotes these words, it is opportune for us to clarify the meaning of that original unity, which has its roots in the fact of the creation of man as male and female.

The narrative of the first chapter of Genesis does not know the problem of man's original solitude: man, in fact, is "male and female" right from the beginning. The Yahwist text of the second chapter, on the contrary, authorizes us, in a way, to think first only of the man since, by means of the body, he belongs to the visible world, but goes beyond it; then, it makes us think of the same man, but through the dualism of sex.

Corporality and sexuality are not completely identified. Although the human body, in its normal constitution, bears within it the signs of sex and is, by its nature, male or female, the fact, however, that man is a "body" belongs to the structure of the personal subject more deeply than the fact that he is in his somatic constitution also male or female. Therefore, the meaning of original solitude, which can be referred simply to "man," is substantially prior to the meaning of original unity. The latter, in fact, is based on masculinity and femininity, as if on two different "incarnations," that is, on two ways of "being a body" of the same human being, created "in the image of God" (Gn. 1:27).

DIALOGUE BETWEEN MAN AND GOD-CREATOR

2. Following the Yahwist text, in which the creation of woman was described separately (Gn. 2:21-22), we must have before our eyes, at the same time, that "image of God" of the first narrative of creation. The second narrative keeps, in language and in style, all the characteristics of the Yahwist text. The way of narrating agrees with the way of thinking and expressing oneself of the period to which the text belongs.

It can be said, following the contemporary philosophy of religion and that of language, that the language in question is a mythical one. In this case, in fact, the term "myth" does not designate a fabulous content, but merely an archaic way of expressing a deeper content. Without any difficulty, we discover, under the layer of the ancient narrative, that content, which is really marvelous as regards the qualities and the condensation of the truths contained in it.

Let us add that the second narrative of the creation of man keeps, up to a certain point, the form of a dialogue between man and God-Creator, and that is manifested above all in that stage in which man ('adam) is definitively created as male and female ('is-'issah).[1] The creation takes place almost simultaneously in two dimensions: the action of God-Yahweh who creates occurs in correlation with the process of human consciousness.

ANALOGY OF SLEEP

3. So, therefore, God-Yahweh says: "It is not good that the man should be alone; I will make him a helper fit for him" (Gn. 2:18). At the same time the man confirms his own solitude (Gn. 2:20). Next we read: "So the Lord God caused a deep sleep to fall upon the man, and while he slept took one of his ribs and closed up its place with flesh; and the rib which the Lord God had taken from the man he made into a woman" (Gn. 2:21-22). Taking into considera-

tion the specificity of the language, it must be recognized in the first place that that sleep in the Genesis account in which the man is immersed, thanks to God-Yahweh, in preparation for the new creative act, gives us food for thought.

Against the background of contemporary mentality, accustomed—through analysis of the subconscious—to connecting sexual contents with the world of dreams, that sleep may bring forth a particular association.[2] However, the Bible narrative seems to go beyond the dimension of man's subconscious. If we admit, moreover, a significant difference of vocabulary, we can conclude that the man *('adam)* falls into that "sleep" in order to wake up "male" and "female." In fact, for the first time in Genesis 2:23 we come across the distinction *'is-issah.* Perhaps, therefore, the analogy of sleep indicates here not so much a passing from consciousness to subconsciousness, as a specific return to non-being (sleep contains an element of annihilation of man's conscious existence), that is, to the moment preceding the creation, in order that, through God's creative initiative, solitary "man" may emerge from it again in his double unity as male and female.[3]

In any case, in the light of the context of Genesis 2:18-20, there is no doubt that man falls into that "sleep" with the desire of finding a being like himself. If, by analogy with sleep, we can speak here also of a dream, we must say that that biblical archetype allows us to admit as the content of that dream a "second self," which is also personal and equally referred to the situation of original solitude, that is, to the whole of that process of the stabilization of human identity in relation to living beings (*animalia*) as a whole, since it is the process of man's "differentiation" from this environment. In this way, the circle of the solitude of the man-person is broken, because the first "man" awakens from his sleep as "male and female."

THE SAME HUMANITY

4. The woman is made "with the rib" that God-Yahweh had taken from the man. Considering the archaic, metaphorical and figurative way of expressing the thought, we can establish that it is a question here of homogeneity of the whole being of both. This homogeneity concerns above all the body, the somatic structure, and is confirmed also by the man's first words to the woman who has been created: "This at last is bone of my bones and flesh of my flesh" (Gn. 2:23).[4] And yet the words quoted refer also to the humanity of the male-man. They must be read in the context of the affirmations made before the creation of the woman, in which, although the "incarnation" of the man does not yet exist, she is defined as "a helper fit for him" (cf. Gn. 2:18 and 2:20).[5] In this way, therefore, the woman is created, in a sense, on the basis of the same humanity.

Somatic homogeneity, in spite of the difference in constitution bound up with the sexual difference, is so evident that the man (male), on waking up from the genetic sleep, expresses it at once, when he says: "This at last is bone of my bones and flesh of my flesh; she shall be called Woman, because she was taken out of Man" (Gn. 2:23). In this way the man (male) manifests for the first time joy and even exaltation, for which he had no reason before, owing to the lack of a being like himself. Joy in the other human being, in the second "self," dominates in the words spoken by the man (male) on seeing the woman (female). All that helps to establish the full meaning of original unity. The words here are few, but each one is of great weight. We must, therefore, take into account—and we will do so also later—the fact that that first woman, "made with the rib...taken from the man (male)," is at once accepted as a fit helper for him.

We shall return to this same subject, that is, the meaning of the original unity of man and of woman in humanity, in the next meditation.

FOOTNOTES

1. The Hebrew term *'adam* expresses the collective concept of the human species, that is, *man* who represents humanity; (the Bible defines the individual using the expression: "son of man," *ben-'adam)*. The contraposition: *'is-'issah* underlines the sexual difference (as in Greek anergyne).

After the creation of the woman, the Bible text continues to call the first man *'adam* (with the definite article), thus expressing his "corporate personality," since he has become "father of mankind," its progenitor and representative, just as Abraham was recognized as "father of believers" and Jacob was identified with Israel—the Chosen People.

2. Adam's sleep (in Hebrew, *tardemah*) is a deep one (Latin: *sopor*), into which man falls without consciousness or dreams (The Bible has another term to define a dream: *halom*); cf. Gn. 15:12; 1 Sm. 26:12.

Freud examines, on the other hand, the content of *dreams* (Latin: *somnium*), which, being formed with physical elements "pushed back into the subconscious" make it possible, in his opinion, to allow the unconscious contents to emerge; the latter, he claims, are, in the last analysis, always sexual.

This idea is, of course, quite alien to the biblical author.

In the theology of the Yahwist author, the sleep into which God caused the first man to fall emphasizes *the exclusivity of God's action* in the work of the creation of the woman; the man had no conscious participation in it. God uses his "rib" only to stress the common nature of man and of woman.

3. *Tardemah* (Italian "torpore," English "sleep") is the term that appears in Holy Scripture when, during sleep or immediately afterwards, extraordinary events are to happen (cf. Gn. 15:12; 1 Sm. 26:12; Is. 29:10; Job 4:13; 33:15). The Septuagint translates *tardemah* with *ekstasis* (ecstasy).

In the Pentateuch *tardemah* appears only once more in a mysterious context: Abram, on God's command, has prepared a sacrifice of animals, driving away birds of prey from them. "As the sun was going down, a *deep sleep* fell on Abram; and lo, *a dread fell upon him*" (Gn. 15:12). Just then God begins to speak and concludes with him a covenant, which is *the summit of the revelation* made to Abram.

This scene is similar in a way to the one in the garden of Gethsemane: Jesus "began to be greatly distressed *and troubled...*" (Mk. 14:33) and found the Apostles "sleeping for sorrow" (Lk. 22:45).

The biblical author admits in the first man a certain sense of privation and solitude ("it is not good that the man should be alone"; "for the man there was not found a helper fit for him"), even if not of fear. Perhaps this state brings about "a sleep caused by sorrow," or perhaps, as in Abram, by "a dread" of non-being; as on the threshold of the work of creation: "The earth was without form and void, and darkness was upon the face of the deep" (Gn. 1:2).

In any case, according to both texts, in which the Pentateuch or rather the Book of Genesis speaks of the deep sleep *(tardemah)*, there takes place a special divine action, that is, a "covenant" pregnant with consequences for the whole history of salvation: Adam begins mankind, Abram the Chosen People.

4. It is interesting to note that for the ancient Sumerians the cuneiform sign to indicate the noun "rib" coincided with the one used to indicate the word "life." As for the Yahwist narrative, according to a certain interpretation of Genesis 2:21, God rather covers the rib with flesh (instead of closing up its place with flesh) and in this way "makes" the woman, who comes from the "flesh and bones" of the first man (male).

In biblical language this is a definition of consanguinity or descent from the same lineage (e.g., cf. Genesis 29:14): the woman belongs to the same species as the man, different from the other living beings created before.

In biblical anthropology, "bones" express a very important element of the body; since for the Jews there was no precise distinction between "body" and "soul" (the body was considered an exterior manifestation of the personality), "bones" meant simply, by synecdoche, the human "being" (cf., for example, Psalm 139:15: "my frame was not hidden from thee"; in Italian "Non ti erano nascoste le mie ossa [bones]").

"Bone of my bones" can therefore be understood, in the relational sense, as "being of my being"; "flesh of my flesh" means that, though she has different physical characteristics, the woman has the same personality as the man possesses.

In the first man's "nuptial song," the expression "bone of my bones, flesh of my flesh" is a form of superlative, stressed, moreover, by the repetition of "this," "she" (in Italian there are three feminine forms: "questa," "essa," "la").

5. It is difficult to translate exactly the Hebrew expression *cezer kenegdô,* which is translated in various ways in European languages, for example:
Latin: "Adiutorium ei conveniens sicut oportebat iuxta eum";

German: "eine Hilfe..., die ihm entspricht";
French: "égal vis-à-vis de lui";
Italian: "un aiuto che gli sia simile"
Spanish: "como él que le ayude";
English: "a helper fit for him";
Polish: "Odopowicdnia alla niego pomoc."

Since the term *"aiuto"* (help) seems to suggest the concept of "complementarity," or better, of "exact correspondence," the term *"simile"* is connected rather with that of "similarity," but in a different sense from man's likeness to God.

By the Communion of Persons Man Becomes the Image of God

General audience of November 14, 1979.

1. Following the narrative of the Book of Genesis, we have seen that the "definitive" creation of man consists in the creation of the unity of two beings. Their unity denotes above all the identity of human nature; the duality, on the other hand, manifests what, on the basis of this identity, constitutes the masculinity and femininity of created man. This ontological dimension of unity and duality has, at the same time, an axiological meaning. From the text of Genesis 2:23 and from the whole context it is clearly seen that man was created as a particular value before God ("God saw everything that he had made, and behold, it was very good": Gn. 1:31), but also as a particular value for the man himself: first, because he is "man"; second, because the "woman" is for the man, and vice versa, the "man" is for the woman.

While the first chapter of Genesis expresses this value in a purely theological form (and indirectly a metaphysical one), the second chapter, on the other hand, reveals, so to speak, the first circle of the experience lived by man as value. This experience is already inscribed in the meaning of original solitude, and then in the whole narrative of the creation of man as male and female. The concise text of Genesis 2:23, which contains the words of the first man at the sight of the woman created, "taken out of him," can be considered the biblical prototype of the Canticle of Canticles. And if it is possible to read impressions and emotions through words so remote, one might also venture to say that the depth and force of this first and "original" emotion of the male-man in the presence of the humanity of the woman, and at the same time in the presence of the femininity of the other human being, seems something unique and unrepeatable.

UNITY IN "COMMUNION OF PERSONS"

2. In this way the meaning of man's original unity, through masculinity and femininity, is expressed as an overcoming of the frontier of solitude, and at the same time as an affirmation—with regard to both human beings—of everything that constitutes "man" in solitude. In the Bible narrative, solitude is the way that leads to that unity which, following Vatican II, we can define as *communio personarum*.[1]

As we have already seen before, man, in his original solitude, acquires a personal consciousness in the process of "distinction" from all living beings *(animalia)* and at the same time, in this solitude, opens up to a being akin to himself, defined in Genesis (2:18 and 20) as "a helper fit for him." This opening is no less decisive for the person of man; in fact, it is perhaps even more decisive than the "distinction" itself. Man's solitude, in the Yahwist narrative, is presented to us not only as the first discovery of the characteristic transcendence peculiar to the person, but also as the discovery of an adequate relationship "to" the person, and therefore as an opening and expectation of a "communion of persons."

The term "community" could also be used here, if it were not generic and did not have so many meanings. *"Communio"* expresses more and with greater precision, since it indicates precisely that "help" which is derived, in a sense, from the very fact of existing as a person "beside" a person. In the Bible narrative this fact becomes *eo ipso*—in itself—the existence of the person "for" the person, since man in his original solitude was, in a way, already in this relationship. That is confirmed, in a negative sense, precisely by this solitude.

Furthermore, the communion of persons could be formed only on the basis of a "double solitude" of man and of woman, that is, as their meeting in their "distinction" from the world of living beings *(animalia)*, which gave them both the possibility of being and existing in a special reciprocity. The concept of "help" also expresses this reciprocity in existence, which no other living being could have ensured. Indispensable for this reciprocity was all that constituted the foundation of the solitude of each of them, and therefore also self-knowledge and self-determination, that is, subjectivity and consciousness of the meaning of one's own body.

IMAGE OF INSCRUTABLE DIVINE COMMUNION

3. The narrative of the creation of man, in the first chapter, affirms right from the beginning and directly that man was created in the image of God as male and female. The narrative of the second chapter, on the other hand, does not speak of the "image of God"; but it reveals, in its own way, that the complete and definitive creation of "man" (subjected first to the experience of original solitude) is expressed in giving life to that *communio personarum* that man and woman form. In this way, the Yahwist narrative agrees with the content of the first narrative.

If, vice versa, we wish to draw also from the narrative of the Yahwist text the concept of "image of God," we can then deduce that man became the "image and likeness" of God not only through his own humanity, but also through the communion of persons which man and woman form right from the beginning. The function of the image is to reflect the one who is the model, to reproduce its own prototype. Man becomes the image of God not so much in the moment of solitude as in the moment of communion. He is, in fact, right "from the beginning" not only an image in which there is reflected the solitude of a Person who rules the world, but also, and essentially, an image of an inscrutable divine communion of Persons.

In this way, the second narrative could also be a preparation for the understanding of the Trinitarian concept of the "image of God," even if the latter appears only in the first narrative. Obviously, that is not without significance also for the theology of the body; in fact, it even constitutes, perhaps, the deepest theological aspect of all that can be said about man. In the mystery of creation—on the basis of the original and constituent "solitude" of his being—man was endowed with a deep unity between what is, humanly and through the body, male in him and what is, equally humanly and through the body, female in him. On all this, right from the beginning, there descended the blessing of fertility, linked with human procreation (cf. Gn. 1:28).

THE BODY REVEALS MAN

4. In this way, we find ourselves almost at the very heart of the anthropological reality that has the name "body." The words of Genesis 2:23 speak of it directly and for the first time in the following terms: "flesh of my flesh and bone of my bones." The male-man utters these words, as if it were only at the sight of the woman that he was able to identify and call by

name what makes them visibly similar to each other, and at the same time what manifests humanity.

In the light of the preceding analysis of all the "bodies," with which man has come into contact and which he has defined, conceptually giving them their name *(animalia)*, the expression "flesh of my flesh" takes on precisely this meaning: the body reveals man. This concise formula already contains everything that human science could ever say about the structure of the body as organism, about its vitality, and its particular sexual physiology, etc. In this first expression of the male-man, "flesh of my flesh," there is also contained a reference to what makes that body truly human, and therefore to what determines man as a person, that is, as a being who, even in all his corporality, is "similar" to God.[2]

MEANING OF UNITY

5. We find ourselves, therefore, almost at the very core of the anthropological reality, the name of which is "body," the human body. However, as can easily be seen, this core is not only anthropological, but also essentially theological. The theology of the body, which, right from the beginning, is bound up with the creation of man in the image of God, becomes, in a way, also the theology of sex, or rather the theology of masculinity and femininity, which has its starting point here, in the Book of Genesis.

The original meaning of unity, to which the words of Genesis 2:24 bear witness, will have in the revelation of God an ample and distant perspective. This unity through the body ("and the two will be one flesh") possesses a multiform dimension: an ethical dimension, as is confirmed by Christ's answer to the Pharisees in Matthew 19 (Mk. 10), and also a sacramental dimension, a strictly theological one, as is proved by St. Paul's words to the Ephesians,[3] which refer also the tradition of the prophets (Hosea, Isaiah, Ezekiel). And this is so because that unity which is realized through the body indicates, right from the beginning, not only the "body," but also the "incarnate" communion of persons—*communio personarum*—and calls for this communion right from the beginning.

Masculinity and femininity express the dual aspect of man's somatic constitution ("This at last is bone of my bones and flesh of my flesh"), and indicate, furthermore, through the same words of Genesis 2:23, the new consciousness of the sense of one's own body: a sense which, it can be said, consists in a mutual enrichment. Precisely this consciousness, through which humanity is formed again as the communion of persons, seems to be the layer which in the narrative of the creation of man (and in the revelation of the body contained in it) is deeper than his very somatic structure as male and female. In any case, this structure is presented right from the beginning

with a deep consciousness of human corporality and sexuality, and that establishes an
inalienable norm for the understanding of man
on the theological plane.

FOOTNOTES

1. "But God did not create man a solitary being. From
the beginning 'male and female he created them' (Gn. 1:17).
This partnership of man and woman constitutes the first
form of communion between persons" (*Gaudium et spes*,
no. 12).

2. The dualistic contraposition "soul-body" does not
appear in the conception of the most ancient books of the
Bible. As has already been stressed (cf. *L'Osservatore
Romano*, English edition, November 5, 1979, page 15,
note 1), we can speak rather of a complementary combina-
tion "body-life." The body is the expression of man's personality, and if it does not fully exhaust this concept, it
must be understood in biblical language as *pars pro toto*; cf.
for example: "Flesh and blood has not revealed this to you,
but my Father..." (Mt. 16:17), that is: it was not a *man* who
revealed it to you.

3. "For no man ever hates his own flesh, but nourishes
it and cherishes it, as Christ does the church, because we
are members of his body. For this reason a man shall leave
his father and mother and be joined to his wife, and the two
shall become one flesh. This mystery is a profound one, and
I am saying that it refers to Christ and the church" (Eph.
5:29-32).

This will be the subject of our reflections in the part
entitled "The Sacrament."

Marriage Is One and Indissoluble in the First Chapters of Genesis

General audience of November 21, 1979.

1. Let us recall that Christ, when questioned about the unity and indissolubility of marriage, referred to what was "in the beginning." He quoted the words written in the first chapters of Genesis. We are trying, therefore, in the course of these reflections, to penetrate the specific meaning of these words and these chapters.

The meaning of the original unity of man, whom God created "male and female," is obtained (particularly in the light of Genesis 2:23) by knowing man in the entire endowment of his being, that is, in all the riches of that mystery of creation, on which theological anthropology is based. This knowledge, that is, the study of the human identity of the one who, at the beginning, is "alone," must always pass through duality, "communion."

Let us recall the passage of Genesis 2:23: "Then the man said, 'This at last is bone of my bones and flesh of my flesh; she shall be called

Woman, because she was taken out of Man.' "
In the light of this text, we understand that
knowledge of man passes through masculinity
and femininity, which are, as it were, two "incarnations" of the same metaphysical solitude,
before God and the world—two ways, as it were,
of "being a body" and at the same time a man,
which complete each other—two complementary dimensions, as it were, of self-consciousness and self-determination and, at the same
time, two complementary ways of being conscious of the meaning of the body.

As Genesis 2:23 already shows, femininity
finds itself, in a sense, in the presence of masculinity, while masculinity is confirmed through
femininity. Precisely the function of sex, which
is, in a sense, "a constituent part of the person"
(not just "an attribute of the person"), proves
how deeply man, with all his spiritual solitude,
with the uniqueness, never to be repeated, of
his person, is constituted by the body as "he"
or "she." The presence of the feminine element,
alongside the male element and together with
it, signifies an enrichment for man in the whole
perspective of his history, including the history of salvation. All this teaching on unity
has already been expressed originally in
Genesis 2:23.

REDISCOVER THE MYSTERY
OF CREATION

2. The unity of which Genesis 2:24 speaks
("they become one flesh"), is undoubtedly what

is expressed and realized in the conjugal act. The biblical formulation, extremely concise and simple, indicates sex, femininity and masculinity, as that characteristic of man—male and female—which permits them, when they become "one flesh," to submit at the same time their whole humanity to the blessing of fertility. However, the whole context of the lapidary formulation does not permit us to stop at the surface of human sexuality, does not allow us to deal with the body and sex outside the full dimension of man and of the "communion of persons," but obliges us right from the beginning to see the fullness and depth characteristic of this unity, which man and woman must constitute in the light of the revelation of the body.

Therefore, first of all, the perspective expression which says: "a man cleaves to his wife" so intimately that "they become one flesh," always induces us to refer to what the biblical text expresses previously with regard to the union in humanity, which binds the woman and the man in the very mystery of creation. The words of Genesis 2:23, just analyzed, explain this concept in a particular way. Man and woman, uniting with each other (in the conjugal act) so closely as to become "one flesh," rediscover, so to speak, every time and in a special way, the mystery of creation. They return in this way to that union in humanity ("flesh of my flesh and bone of my bones") which allows them to recognize each other and, like the first time, to call each other by name.

This means reliving, in a sense, the original virginal value of man, which emerges from the mystery of his solitude before God and in the midst of the world. The fact that they become "one flesh" is a powerful bond established by the Creator, through which they discover their own humanity, both in its original unity, and in the duality of a mysterious mutual attraction.

Sex, however, is something more than the mysterious power of human corporality, which acts almost by virtue of instinct. At the level of man and in the mutual relationship of persons, sex expresses an ever new surpassing of the limit of man's solitude that is inherent in the constitution of his body, and determines its original meaning. This surpassing always contains within it a certain assumption of the solitude of the body of the second "self" as one's own.

CHOICE ESTABLISHES PACT

3. Therefore, it is bound up with choice. The very formulation of Genesis 2:24 indicates not only that human beings, created as man and woman, were created for unity, but also that precisely this unity, through which they become "one flesh," has right from the beginning a character of union derived from a choice. We read, in fact: "a man leaves his father and mother and cleaves to his wife." If the man belongs "by nature" to his father and

mother, by virtue of procreation, he, on the other hand, "cleaves" by choice to his wife (or she to her husband).

The text of Genesis 2:24 defines this character of the conjugal bond with reference to the first man and the first woman, but at the same time, it does so also in the perspective of the whole earthly future of man. Therefore, in His time, Christ will appeal to that text, as equally relevant in His age. Formed in the image of God, also inasmuch as they form a true communion of persons, the first man and the first woman must constitute the beginning and the model of that communion for all men and women, who, in any period, are united so intimately as to be "one flesh."

The body, which through its own masculinity or femininity right from the beginning helps both ("a helper fit for him") to find themselves in communion of persons, becomes, in a particular way, the constituent element of their union, when they become husband and wife. This takes place, however, through a mutual choice. It is the choice that establishes the conjugal pact between persons,[1] who becomes "one flesh" only on this basis.

SELF-GIVING OF PERSONS

4. That corresponds to the structure of man's solitude, and in actual fact to the "two-fold solitude." Choice, as the expression of self-determination, rests on the foundation of his

self-consciousness. Only on the basis of the structure peculiar to man is he "a body" and, through the body, also male and female. When they both unite so closely as to become "one flesh," their conjugal union presupposes a mature consciousness of the body. In fact, it bears within it a particular consciousness of the meaning of that body in the mutual self-giving of the persons.

In this sense, too, Genesis 2:24 is a perspective text. It proves, in fact, that in every conjugal union of man and woman there is discovered again the same original consciousness of the unifying significance of the body in its masculinity and femininity. With that the biblical text indicates, at the same time, that in each of these unions there is renewed, in a way, the mystery of creation in all its original depth and vital power. "Taken out of man" as "flesh of his flesh," woman subsequently becomes, as "wife" and through her motherhood, mother of the living (cf. Gn. 3:20), since her motherhood also has its origin in him. Procreation is rooted in creation, and every time, in a sense, reproduces its mystery.

5. A special reflection: "Knowledge and procreation" will be devoted to this subject. In it, it will be necessary to refer further to other elements of the biblical text. The analysis made hitherto of the meaning of the original unity proves in what way that unity of man and woman, inherent in the mystery of creation, is

"from the beginning" also given as a commitment in the perspective of all following times.

FOOTNOTE

1. "The intimate partnership of life and the love which constitutes the married state has been established by the Creator and endowed by Him with its own proper laws: it is rooted in the contract of its partners, that is, in their irrevocable personal consent" (GS 48).

Meaning of
Original Human Experiences

General audience of December 12, 1979.

1. It can be said that the analysis of the first chapters of Genesis forces us, in a way, to reconstruct the elements that constitute man's original experience. In this sense, the Yahwist text is, by its character, a special source. Speaking of original human experiences, we have in mind not so much their distance in time, as rather their basic significance. The important thing, therefore, is not that these experiences belong to man's prehistory (to his "theological prehistory"), but that they are always at the root of every human experience. That is true, even if, in the evolution of ordinary human existence, not much attention is paid to these essential experiences. They are, in fact, so intermingled with the ordinary things of life that we do not generally notice their extraordinary character.

On the basis of the analyses carried out up to now, we have already been able to realize that what we called at the beginning "revelation of the body," helps us somehow to discover the extraordinary side of what is ordinary. That is possible because the revelation (the original one, which found expression first in the Yahwist account of Genesis 2-3, then in the text of Genesis 1) takes into consideration precisely these primordial experiences in which there appears almost completely the absolute originality of what the male-female human being is: as a man, that is, also through his body. Man's experience of his body, as we discover it in the biblical text quoted, is certainly on the threshold of the whole subsequent "historical" experience. It also seems to rest, however, at such an ontological depth that man does not perceive it in his own everyday life, even if at the same time, and in a certain way, he presupposes it and postulates it as part of the process of formation of his own image.

2. Without this introductory reflection, it would be impossible to define the meaning of original nakedness and tackle the analysis of Genesis 2:25, which runs as follows: "And the man and his wife were both naked, and were not ashamed." At first sight, the introduction of this detail, apparently a secondary one in the Yahwist account of man's creation, may seem something inadequate or misplaced. One would think that the passage quoted cannot bear comparison with what has been dealt with in the preceding verses and that, in a way, it goes beyond the context. However, this judgment does not stand up to a deeper analysis. In fact, Genesis 2:25 presents one of the key-elements

of the original revelation, as decisive as the other texts of Genesis (2:20 and 2:23), which have already enabled us to define the meaning of man's original solitude and original unity. To these is added, as the third element, the meaning of original nakedness, clearly stressed in the context; and, in the first biblical draft of anthropology, it is not something accidental. On the contrary, it is precisely the key for its full and complete understanding.

3. It is evident that precisely this element of the ancient biblical text makes a specific contribution to the theology of the body, a contribution that absolutely cannot be ignored. Further analyses will confirm this. But, before undertaking them, I take the liberty of pointing out that the very text of Genesis 2:25 expressly requires that the reflections on the theology of the body should be connected with the dimension of man's personal subjectivity; it is within the latter, in fact, that consciousness of the meaning of the body develops. Genesis 2:25 speaks about it far more directly than other parts of that Yahwist text, which we have already defined as the first recording of human consciousness.

The sentence, according to which the first human beings, man and woman, "were naked" and yet "were not ashamed," unquestionably describes their state of consciousness; in fact, their mutual experience of the body—that is, the experience on the part of the man of the femininity that is revealed in the nakedness of the body and, reciprocally, the similiar experience of masculinity on the part of the woman. By saying that "they were not ashamed," the author tries to describe this mutual experience of the body with the greatest precision possible for him. It can be said that this type of precision reflects a basic experience of man in the "common" and prescientific sense, but it also corresponds to the requirements of anthropology and in particular of contemporary anthropology, which likes to refer to so-called fundamental experiences, such as the experience of shame.[1]

4. Referring here to the precision of the account, such as was possible for the author of the Yahwist text, we are led to consider the degrees of experience of "historical" man, laden with the inheritance of sin, degrees, however, which methodically start precisely from the state of original innocence. Previously we have already seen that, referring to "the beginning" (which we have subjected here to successive contextual analyses), Christ indirectly establishes the idea of continuity and connection between those two states, as if allowing us to move back from the threshold of man's "historical" sinfulness to his original innocence. Precisely Genesis 2:25 makes it particularly necessary to cross that threshold.

It is easy to point out how this passage, together with the meaning of original nakedness inherent in it, takes its place in the contextual setting of the Yahwist narrative. After some verses, in fact, the same author writes: "Then the eyes of both were opened, and they knew that they were naked; and they sewed fig leaves together and made themselves aprons" (Gn. 3:7). The adverb "then" indicates a new moment and a new situation following upon the breaking of the first covenant; it is a situation that follows the failure of the test connected with the tree of the knowledge of good and evil, which at the same time constituted the first test of "obedience," that is, listening to the Word in all its truth and accepting love, according to the fullness of the demands of the creative Will. This new moment or new situation also implies a new content and a new quality of experience of the body, so that it can no longer be said: "they were naked, but were not ashamed." Here, therefore, shame is an experience that is not only original, but a "boundary" one.

5. The difference of formulations that divides Genesis 2:25 from Genesis 3:7 is, therefore, a significant one. In the first case, "they were naked, but they were not ashamed"; in the second case, "they knew that they were naked." Does that mean that, to begin with, "they did not know that they were naked"? That they did not see the nakedness of each other's body? The significant change testified by the biblical text about the experience of shame (of which Genesis speaks again, particularly in 3:10-12), takes place at a deeper level than the pure and simple use of the sense of sight.

A comparative analysis between Genesis 2:25 and Genesis 3 leads necessarily to the conclusion that it is not a question here of passing from "not knowing" to "knowing," but of a radical change of the meaning of the original nakedness of the woman before the man and of the man before the woman. It emerges from their conscience, as a fruit of the tree of the knowledge of good and evil: "Who told you that you were naked? Have you eaten of the tree of which I commanded you not to eat?" (Gn. 3:11)

This change directly concerns the experience of the meaning of one's body before the Creator and creatures. That is confirmed subsequently by the man's words: "I heard the sound of you in the garden, and I was afraid, because I was naked; and I hid myself" (Gn. 3:10). But in particular that change, which the Yahwist text portrays so concisely and dramatically, concerns directly—perhaps in the most direct way possible—the man-woman, femininity-masculinity relationship.

6. We will have to return again to the analysis of this change in other parts of our further reflections. Now, having arrived at that border which crosses the sphere of the "beginning" to which Christ referred, we should ask ourselves if it is possible to reconstruct, in some way, the original meaning of nakedness, which, in the Book of Genesis, constitutes the immediate context of the doctrine about the unity of the human being as male and female. That seems possible, if we take as reference

point the experience of shame as it was clearly presented in the ancient biblical text as a "liminal" experience.

We shall seek to attempt this reconstruction in our following meditations.

FOOTNOTE

1. Cf., for example: M. Scheler, *Über Scham und Schamgefühl*, Halle 1914; Fr. Sawicki, *Fenomenologia wstydiiwosci* (Phenomenology of shame), Krakow 1949; and also K. Wojtyla, *Milosc i odpowiedzialnosc*, Krakow 1962, pp. 165-185 (in Italian: *Amore e responsabilita*, Rome 1978, II ed., pp. 161-178).

Fullness of
Interpersonal Communication

General audience of December 19, 1979.

1. What is shame and how can we explain its absence in the state of original innocence, in the very depth of the mystery of the creation of man as male and female? From contemporary analyses of shame—and in particular sexual modesty—we can deduce the complexity of this fundamental experience, in which man expresses himself as a person according to his own specific structure. In the experience of shame, the human being experiences fear with regard to his "second self" (as, for example, woman before man), and this is substantially fear for his own "self." With shame, the human being manifests almost "instinctively" the need of affirmation and acceptance of this "self," according to its rightful value. He experiences it at the same time both within himself, and externally, before the "other." It can therefore be said that shame is a complex experience also in the sense that, almost keeping one human being away from the other (woman from man), it

seeks at the same time to draw them closer personally, creating a suitable basis and level in order to do so.

For the same reason, it has a fundamental significance as regards the formation of *ethos* in human society, and in particular in the man-woman relationship. The analysis of shame clearly indicates how deeply it is rooted precisely in mutual relations, how exactly it expresses the essential rules for the "communion of persons," and likewise how deeply it touches the dimension of man's original "solitude." The appearance of "shame" in the subsequent biblical narration of Chapter 3 of Genesis has a pluri-dimensional significance, and it will be opportune to resume the analysis in due time.

What does its original absence mean, on the other hand, in Genesis 2:25: "They were both naked and were not ashamed"?

MISLEADING ANALOGIES

2. It is necessary to establish, in the first place, that it is a question of a real non-presence of shame, and not a lack of underdevelopment of it. We cannot in any way sustain here a "primitivization" of its meaning. Therefore the text of Genesis 2:25 does not only exclude decisively the possibility of thinking of a "lack of shame" or immodesty, but even more excludes the possibility of explaining it by means of analogy with some positive human experiences, such as, for example, those of childhood or of the life of so-called primitive peoples. These

analogies are not only insufficient, but they can even be misleading. The words of Genesis 2:25, "they were not ashamed," do not express a lack, but, on the contrary, serve to indicate a particular fullness of consciousness and experience, above all fullness of understanding of the meaning of the body, bound up with the fact that "they were naked."

That this is how the text quoted is to be understood and interpreted is testified by the continuation of the Yahwist narrative, in which the appearance of shame, and in particular of sexual modesty, is connected with the loss of that original fullness. Taking, therefore, the experience of shame as a "borderline" experience, we must ask ourselves to what fullness of conscience and experience, and in particular to what fullness of understanding of the meaning of the body, the meaning of original nakedness, of which Genesis 2:25 speaks, corresponds.

FULLNESS OF CONSCIOUSNESS

3. To answer this question, it is necessary to keep in mind the analytical process carried out so far, which has its basis in the Yahwist passage as a whole. In this context, man's original solitude is manifested as "non-identification" of his own humanity with the world of living beings (*animalia*) that surround him.

This "non-identification," following upon the creation of man as male and female, makes way for the happy discovery of one's own humanity "with the help" of the other human being; thus the man recognizes and finds again his own humanity "with the help" of the woman (Gn. 2:25). At the same time, this act of theirs realizes a perception of the world, which is carried out directly through the body ("flesh of my flesh"). It is the direct and visible source of the experience that arrives at establishing their unity in humanity. It is not difficult to understand, therefore, that nakedness corresponds to that fullness of consciousness of the meaning of the body, deriving from the typical perception of the senses.

One can think of this fullness in categories of truth of being or of reality, and it can be said that man and woman were originally given to each other precisely according to this truth, since "they were naked." In the analysis of the meaning of original nakedness, this dimension absolutely cannot be disregarded. This participating in perception of the world—in its "exterior" aspect—is a direct and almost spontaneous fact, prior to any "critical" complication of knowledge and of human experience and is seen as closely connected with the experience of the meaning of the human body. The original innocence of "knowledge" could already be perceived in this way.

MEANING OF COMMUNICATION

4. However, it is not possible to determine the meaning of original nakedness considering only man's participation in exterior perception

of the world; it is not possible to establish it without going down into the depths of man. Genesis 2:25 introduces us specifically to this level and wants us to seek there the original innocence of knowing. In fact, it is with the dimension of human interiority that it is necessary to explain and measure that particular fullness of interpersonal communication, thanks to which man and woman "were naked and were not ashamed."

The concept of "communication," in our conventional language, has been practically alienated from its deepest, original semantic matrix. It is connected mainly with the sphere of the media, that is, for the most part, products that serve for understanding, exchange, and bringing closer together. It can be supposed, on the other hand, that, in its original and deeper meaning, "communication" was and is directly connected with subjects, who "communicate" precisely on the basis of the "common union" that exists between them, both to reach and to express a reality that is peculiar and pertinent only to the sphere of person-subjects.

In this way, the human body acquires a completely new meaning, which cannot be placed on the plane of the remaining "external" perception of the world. It expresses, in fact, the person in his ontological and existential concreteness, which is something more than the "individual," and therefore expresses the personal human "self," which derives its "exterior" perception from within.

MAN'S VISION OF GOD

5. The whole biblical narrative, and in particular the Yahwist text, shows that the body through its own visibility manifests man and, manifesting him, acts as intermediary, that is, enables man and woman, right from the beginning, "to communicate" with each other according to that *communio personarum* willed by the Creator precisely for them. Only this dimension, it seems, enables us to understand in the right way the meaning of original nakedness. In this connection, any "naturalistic" criterion is bound to fail, while, on the contrary, the "personalistic" criterion can be of great help. Genesis 2:25 certainly speaks of something extraordinary, which is outside the limits of the shame known through human experience and which at the same time decides the particular fullness of interpersonal communication, rooted at the very heart of that *communio*, which is thus revealed and developed. In this connection, the words "they were not ashamed" can mean *(in sensu obliquo)* only an original depth in affirming what is inherent in the person, what is "visibly" female and male, through which the "personal intimacy" of mutual communication in all its radical simplicity and purity is constituted. To this fullness of "exterior" perception, expressed by means of physical nakedness, there corresponds the "interior" fullness of man's vision in God, that is, according to the measure of the "image of God" (cf. Gn. 1:17). According to this measure, man

"is" really naked ("they were naked": Gn. 2:25),[1] even before realizing it (cf. Gn. 3:7-10).

We shall still have to complete the analysis of this important text during the meditations that follow.

FOOTNOTE

1. God, according to the words of Holy Scripture, penetrates the creature, who is completely "naked" before Him: "And before him no creature is hidden, but all are open *(pánta gymná)* and laid bare to the eyes of him with whom we have to do" (Heb. 4:13). This characteristic belongs in particular to Divine Wisdom: "Wisdom... because of her pureness pervades and penetrates all things" (Wis. 7:24).

Creation as Fundamental and Original Gift

General audience of January 2, 1980.

1. Let us return to the analysis of the text of Genesis (2:25), started some weeks ago. ("And the man and his wife were both naked and were not ashamed." Gn. 2:25)

According to this passage, the man and the woman see themselves, as it were, through the mystery of creation; they see themselves in this way, before knowing "that they are naked." This seeing each other is not just a participation in "exterior" perception of the world, but has also an interior dimension of participation in the vision of the Creator Himself—that vision of which the Elohist text speaks several times: "God saw everything that he had made, and behold, it was very good" (Gn. 1:31).

SEEING EACH OTHER

"Nakedness" signifies the original good of God's vision. It signifies all the simplicity and fullness of the vision through which the "pure" value of humanity as male and female, the

"pure" value of the body and of sex, is manifested. The situation that is indicated, in such
a concise and at the same time inspiring way,
by the original revelation of the body as seen
in particular by Genesis 2:25, does not know
an interior rupture and opposition between
what is spiritual and what is sensible, just
as it does not know a rupture and opposition
between what constitutes the person humanly
and what in man is determined by sex: what is
male and female.

Seeing each other, as if through the very
mystery of creation, man and woman see each
other even more fully and distinctly than
through the sense of sight itself, that is, through
the eyes of the body. They see and know each
other, in fact, with all the peace of the interior
gaze, which creates precisely the fullness of
the intimacy of persons.

GIFT FOR EACH OTHER

If "shame" brings with it a specific limita-
tion in seeing by means of the eyes of the body,
this takes place above all because personal
intimacy is, as it were, disturbed and almost
"threatened" by this sight. According to Genesis 2:25, the man and the woman "were not
ashamed": seeing and knowing each other
in all the peace and tranquility of the interior
gaze, they "communicate" in the fullness of
humanity, which is manifested in them as reciprocal complementariness precisely because
they are "male" and "female." At the same

time, they "communicate" on the basis of that communion of persons in which, through femininity and masculinity, they become a gift for each other. In this way they reach in reciprocity a special understanding of the meaning of their own body.

The original meaning of nakedness corresponds to that simplicity and fullness of vision in which understanding of the meaning of the body comes about, as it were, at the very heart of their community-communion. We will call it "nuptial." The man and the woman in Genesis 2:23-25 emerge, precisely at the "beginning," with this consciousness of the meaning of their body. That deserves a careful analysis.

BEARING A DIVINE IMAGE

2. If the narrative of the creation of man in the two versions, the Elohist and the Yahwist, enables us to establish the original meaning of solitude, unity and nakedness, it thereby enables us also to find ourselves on the ground of an adequate anthropology, which tries to understand and interpret man in what is essentially human.[1]

The Bible texts contain the essential elements of this anthropology, which are manifested in the theological context of the "image of God." This concept conceals within it the very root of the truth about man, revealed through that "beginning," to which Christ refers in the talk with the Pharisees (cf. Mt. 19:3-9), when He treats of the creation of human male and female. It must be recalled that all the analyses we make here are connected, at least indirectly, precisely with these words of His. Man, whom God created "male and female," bears the divine image imprinted on his body "from the beginning"; man and woman constitute, as it were, two different ways of the human "being a body" in the unity of that image.

Now, it is opportune to turn again to those fundamental words which Christ used, that is, the word "created" and the subject "Creator," introducing in the considerations made so far a new dimension, a new criterion of understanding and interpretation, which we will call "hermeneutics of the gift." The dimension of the gift decides the essential truth and depth of meaning of the original solitude-unity-nakedness. It is also at the very heart of the mystery of creation, which enables us to construct the theology of the body "from the beginning," but demands, at the same time, that we should construct it just in this way.

CALLS INTO EXISTENCE

3. The word "created," on Christ's lips, contains the same truth that we find in the Book of Genesis. The first account of creation repeats this word several times, from Genesis 1:1 ("In the beginning God created the heavens and the earth") to Genesis 1:27 ("So God created man in his own image").[2] God reveals Himself above all as Creator. Christ refers to that fundamental

revelation contained in the Book of Genesis. In it, the concept of creation has all its depth—not only metaphysical, but also fully theological.

The Creator is He who "calls to existence from nothingness," and who establishes the world in existence and man in the world, because He "is love" (1 Jn. 4:8). Actually, we do not find this word in the narrative of creation; however, this narrative often repeats: "God saw what he had made, and behold, it was very good." Through these words we are led to glimpse in love the divine motive of creation, the source, as it were, from which it springs: only love, in fact, gives a beginning to good and delights in good (cf. 1 Cor. 13). The creation, therefore, as the action of God, signifies not only calling from nothingness to existence and establishing the existence of the world and of man in the world, but it also signifies, according to the first narrative, "beresit bara," giving; a fundamental and "radical" giving, that is, a giving in which the gift comes into being precisely from nothingness.

RELATIONSHIP EMERGES

4. The reading of the first chapters of the book of Genesis introduces us to the mystery of creation, that is, the beginning of the world by the will of God, who is omnipotence and love. Consequently, every creature bears within him the sign of the original and fundamental gift.

At the same time, however, the concept of "giving" cannot refer to a nothingness. It indicates the one who gives and the one who receives the gift, and also the relationship that is established between them. Now, this relationship emerges in the account of creation at the very moment of the creation of man. This relationship is manifested above all by the expression: "God created man in his own image, in the image of God he created him" (Gn. 1:27).

In the narrative of the creation of the visible world, the giving has a meaning only with regard to man. In the whole work of creation, it can be said only of him that a gift was conferred on him: the visible world was created "for him." The biblical account of creation offers us sufficient reasons to understand and interpret in this way: creation is a gift, because there appears in it man who, as the "image of God," is capable of understanding the very meaning of gift in the call from nothingness to existence. And he is capable of answering the Creator with the language of this understanding. Interpreting the narrative of creation with this language, it can be deduced from it that creation constitutes the fundamental and original gift: man appears in creation as the one who received the world as a gift, and *vice versa* it can also be said that the world received man as a gift.

At this point, we must interrupt our analysis. What we have said so far is in very close relationship with all the anthropological problems of the "beginning." Man appears as "created," that is, as the one who, in the midst of the "world," received the other man as a gift. And later we will have to make precisely this dimension of the gift the subject of a deep analysis in order to understand also the meaning of the human body in its rightful extent. This will be the subject of our next meditations.

FOOTNOTES

1. The concept of an "adequate anthropology" has been explained in the text itself as "understanding and interpretation of man in what is essentially human." This concept determines the very principle of reduction, characteristic of the philosophy of man, indicates the limit of this principle, and indirectly excludes the possibility of going beyond this limit. An "adequate" anthropology rests on essentially "human" experience, opposed to the reductionism of the "naturalistic" type, which often goes hand in hand with the evolutionistic theory about the beginnings of man.

2. The Hebrew term *bara*—created, used exclusively to determine the action of God—appears in the account of creation only in v. 1 (creation of the heavens and of the earth), in v. 21 (creation of animals), and in v. 27 (creation of man): here, however, it appears as often as three times. This signifies the fullness and perfection of that act which is the creation of man, male and female. This repetition indicates that the world of creation reached its culminating point here.

Nuptial Meaning
of the Body

General audience of January 9, 1980.

1. Rereading and analyzing the second narrative of creation, that is, the Yahwist text, we must ask ourselves if the first "man" (*'adam)*, in his original solitude, really "lived" the world as a gift, with an attitude in conformity with the actual condition of one who has received a gift, as is seen from the narrative in the first chapter. The second narrative shows us man, in fact, in the garden of Eden (cf. Gn. 2:8); but we must observe that, though in this situation of original happiness, the Creator Himself (God Yahweh) and then also "man," instead of stressing the aspect of the world as a subjectively beatifying gift created for man (cf. the first narrative and in particular Gn. 26:29), point out that man is "alone."

We have already analyzed the meaning of original solitude. Now, however, it is necessary to note that there clearly appears for the first time a certain lack of good: "It is not good that man (male) should be alone"—God Yahweh says—"I will make him a helper..." (Gn. 2:18). The first "man" says the same thing. He, too, after having become thoroughly aware of his own solitude among all living beings on earth, waits for "a helper fit for him" (cf. Gn. 2:20). In fact, none of these beings *(animalia)* offers man the basic conditions, which make it possible to exist in a relationship of mutual giving.

WITH AND FOR SOMEONE

2. In this way, therefore, these two expressions, namely, the adjective "alone" and the noun "helper," seem to be really the key to understand the very essence of the gift at the level of man, as existential content contained in the truth of the "image of God." In fact the gift reveals, so to speak, a particular characteristic of personal existence, or rather, of the very essence of the person. When God Yahweh says that "it is not good that man should be alone" (Gn. 2:18), He affirms that "alone," man does not completely realize this essence. He realizes it only by existing *"with someone"*—and even more deeply and completely: by existing *"for someone."*

This norm of existence as a person is shown in the Book of Genesis as characteristic of creation, precisely by means of the meaning of these two words: "alone" and "helper." It is precisely these words which indicate as fundamental and constitutive for man both the relationship and the communion of persons. The communion of persons means existing in a mutual "for," in a relationship of mutual gift. And this relationship is precisely the fulfillment of "man's" original solitude.

EFFECTED BY LOVE

3. This fulfillment is, in its origin, beatifying. It is certainly implicit in man's original happiness, and constitutes precisely that happiness which belongs to the mystery of creation effected by love, which belongs to the very essence of creative giving. When man—"the male," awakening from the sleep of Genesis, sees man—"the female," drawn from him, he says: "This at last is bone of my bones and flesh of my flesh" (Gen. 2:23). These words express, in a way, the subjectively beatifying beginning of man's existence in the world. Since it took place at the "beginning," this confirms the process of individuation of man in the world, and springs, so to speak, from the very depths of his human solitude, which he lives as a person in the presence of all other creatures and all living beings (animalia).

This "beginning" belongs, therefore, to an adequate anthropology and can always be verified on the basis of the latter. This purely anthropological verification brings us, at the same time, to the subject of the "person" and to the subject of the "body-sex." This simultaneousness is essential. If, in fact, we dealt with sex without the person, the whole adequacy of the anthropology, which we find in the

Book of Genesis, would be destroyed. And for our theological study the essential light of the revelation of the body, which appears so fully in these first affirmations, would then be veiled.

BODY EXPRESSES PERSON

4. There is a deep connection between the mystery of creation, as a gift springing from love, and that beatifying "beginning" of the existence of man as male and female, in the whole truth of their body and their sex, which is the pure and simple truth of communion between persons. When the first man exclaims, at the sight of the woman: "This is bone of my bones, and flesh of my flesh" (Gn. 2:23), he merely affirms the human identity of both. Exclaiming in this way, he seems to say: here is *a body that expresses the "person"!*

Following a preceding passage of the Yahwist text, it can also be said that this "body" reveals the "living soul," such as man became when God Yahweh breathed life into him (cf. Gn. 2:7), as a result of which there began his solitude before all other living beings. Precisely by traversing the depth of that original solitude, man now emerges in the dimension of the mutual gift, the expression of which—and for that very reason the expression of his existence as a person—is the human body in all the original truth of its masculinity and femininity.

The body, which expresses femininity, manifests the reciprocity and communion of persons. It expresses it by means of the gift as the fundamental characteristic of personal existence. This is the body: a witness to creation as a fundamental gift, and so a witness to Love as the source from which this same giving springs. Masculinity-femininity—namely, sex—is the original sign of a creative donation and of an awareness on the part of man, male-female, of a gift lived so to speak in an original way. Such is the meaning with which sex enters the theology of the body.

CALLED "NUPTIAL"

5. That beatifying "beginning" of man's being and existing, as male and female, is connected with the revelation and discovery of the meaning of the body, which can be called "nuptial." If we speak of revelation and at the same time of discovery, we do so in relation to the specificness of the Yahwist text, in which the theological thread is also anthropological, appearing, in fact, as a certain reality consciously lived by man.

We have already observed that the words which express the first joy of man's coming to existence as "male and female" (Gn. 2:23) are followed by the verse which establishes their conjugal unity (Gn. 2:24), and then by the one which testifies to the nakedness of both, without mutual shame (Gn. 2:25). Precisely this significant confrontation enables us to speak of the revelation and at the same time the discovery of the "nuptial" meaning of the body in the very mystery of creation.

This meaning (inasmuch as it is revealed and also conscious, "lived" by man) confirms completely that the creative giving, which springs from Love, has reached the original consciousness of man, becoming an experience of mutual giving, as can already be seen in the archaic text. That nakedness of both progenitors, free from shame, seems also to bear witness to that—perhaps even specifically.

BLESSING OF FERTILITY

6. Genesis 2:24 speaks of the finality of man's masculinity and femininity, in the life of the spouses-parents. Uniting with each other so closely as to become "one flesh," they will subject, in a way, their humanity to the blessing of fertility, namely, "procreation," of which the first narrative speaks (Gn. 1:28). Man comes "into being" with consciousness of this finality of his own masculinity-femininity, that is, of his own sexuality. At the same time, the words of Genesis 2:25: "they were both naked, and were not ashamed," seem to add to this fundamental truth of the meaning of the human body, of its masculinity and femininity, another no less essential and fundamental truth. Man, aware of the procreative capacity of his body and of his sexuality, is at the same time free from the "constraint" of his own body and sex.

That original nakedness, mutual and at the same time not weighed down by shame, expresses this interior freedom of man. Is this what freedom from the "sexual instinct" is? The concept of "instinct" already implies an interior constraint, similar to the instinct that stimulates fertility and procreation in the whole world of living beings (*animalia*). It seems, however, that both texts of the Book of Genesis, the first and the second narrative of the creation of man, connected sufficiently the perspective of procreation with the fundamental characteristic of human existence in the personal sense. Consequently the analogy of the human body and of sex in relation to the world of animals —which we can call analogy "of nature"—is also raised, in a way, in both narratives (though in a different way in each), to the level of "image of God," and to the level of the person and communion between persons.

It will be necessary to dedicate other further analyses to this essential problem. For the conscience of man—also for modern man—it is important to know that in those biblical texts which speak of the "beginning" of man, there is found the revelation of the "nuptial meaning of the body." But it is even more important to establish what this meaning expresses precisely.

The Man-Person Becomes
a Gift in the Freedom of Love

General audience of January 16, 1980.

1. Let us continue today with the analysis of the texts of the Book of Genesis, which we have undertaken according to Christ's line of teaching. Let us recall, in fact, that in the talk about marriage He referred to the "beginning."

The revelation, and at the same time the original discovery of the "nuptial" meaning of the body, consists in presenting man, male and female, in the whole reality and truth of his body and sex ("they were naked") and at the same time in full freedom from any constraint of the body and of sex. The nakedness of our progenitors, interiorly free from shame, seems to bear witness to this. It can be said that, created by Love, that is, endowed in their being with masculinity and femininity, they are both "naked" because they are free with the very freedom of the gift.

This freedom lies precisely at the basis of the nuptial meaning of the body. The human body, with its sex, and its masculinity and femininity seen in the very mystery of creation, is not only a source of fruitfulness and procreation, as in the whole natural order, but includes right "from the beginning" the "nuptial" attribute, that is, the capacity of expressing love: that love precisely in which the man-person becomes a gift and—by means of this gift—fulfills the very meaning of his being and existence. Let us recall here the text of the last Council, where it is declared that man is the only creature in the visible world that God willed "for its own sake," adding that this man "can fully discover his true self only in a sincere giving of himself."[1]

2. The root of that original nakedness free from shame, of which Genesis 2:25 speaks, must be sought precisely in that complete truth about man. Man or woman, in the context of their beatifying "beginning," are free with the very freedom of the gift. In fact, to be able to remain in the relationship of the "sincere gift of themselves" and to become such a gift for each other through the whole of their humanity made of femininity and masculinity (also in relation to that perspective of which Genesis 2:24 speaks), they must be free precisely in this way.

We mean here freedom particularly as mastery of oneself (self-control). From this aspect, it is indispensable in order that man may be able to "give himself," in order that he may become a gift, in order that (referring to the words of the Council) he will be able to "fully discover his true self" in "a sincere giving of himself." Thus the words "they were naked and were not ashamed" can and must be understood as the revelation—and at the same time rediscovery—of freedom, which makes possible and qualifies the "nuptial" sense of the body.

3. Genesis 2:25 says even more, however. In fact, this passage indicates the possibility and the characteristic of this mutual "experience of the body." And it enables us furthermore to identify that nuptial meaning of the body *in actu*. When we read that "they were naked and were not ashamed," we indirectly touch almost the root of it and directly already the fruits. Free interiorly from the constraint of his (her) own body and sex, free with the freedom of the gift, man and woman could enjoy the whole truth, the whole self-evidence of man, just as God Yahweh had revealed these things to them in the mystery of creation.

This truth about man, which the conciliar text states precisely in the words quoted above, has two main emphases. The first affirms that man is the only creature in the world that the Creator willed "for its own sake"; the second consists in saying that this same man, willed by the Creator in this way right from "the beginning," can find himself only in the disinterested giving of himself. Now, this truth about man, which seems in particular to grasp the original condition connected with the very "beginning" of man in the mystery of creation, can be reread—on the basis of the conciliar text—in both directions. This rereading helps us to understand even more the nuptial meaning of the body, which seems inscribed in the original condition of man and woman (according to Genesis 2:23-25) and in particular in the meaning of their original nakedness.

If, as we have noted, at the root of their nakedness there is the interior freedom of the gift—the disinterested gift of oneself—precisely that gift enables them both, man and woman, *to find one another,* since the Creator willed each of them "for his (her) own sake" (cf. *Gaudium et spes,* 24). Thus man, in the first beatifying meeting, finds the woman, and she finds him. In this way he accepts her interiorly; he accepts her as she is willed "for her own sake" by the Creator, as she is constituted in the mystery of the image of God through her femininity; and, reciprocally, she accepts him in the same way, as he is willed "for his own sake" by the Creator, and constituted by him by means of his masculinity. The revelation and the discovery of the "nuptial" meaning of the body consists in this. The Yahwist narrative, and in particular Genesis 2:25, enables us to deduce that man, as male and female, enters the world precisely with this awareness of the meaning of his body, of his masculinity and femininity.

4. The human body, oriented interiorly by the "sincere gift" of the person, reveals not only

its masculinity or femininity on the physical plane, but reveals also such a value and such a beauty as to go beyond the purely physical dimension of "sexuality."[2] In this manner awareness of the nuptial meaning of the body, connected with man's masculinity-femininity, is in a way completed. On the one hand, this meaning indicates a particular capacity of expressing love, in which man becomes a gift; on the other hand, there corresponds to it the capacity and deep availability for the "affirmation of the person," that is, literally, the capacity of living the fact that the other—the woman for the man and the man for the woman—is, by means of the body, someone willed by the Creator "for his (her) own sake," that is, unique and unrepeatable: some one chosen by eternal Love.

The "affirmation of the person" is nothing but acceptance of the gift, which, by means of reciprocity, creates the communion of persons. The latter is constructed from within, comprising also the whole "exteriority" of man, that is, everything that constitutes the pure and simple nakedness of the body in its masculinity and femininity. Then—as we read in Genesis 2:25—man and woman were not ashamed. The biblical expression "were not ashamed" directly indicates "the experience" as a subjective dimension.

5. Precisely in this subjective dimension, as two human "egos" determined by their mascu-

linity and femininity, both of them, man and woman, appear in the mystery of their beatifying "beginning" (We are in the state of man's original innocence and at the same time, original happiness). This appearance is a short one, since it comprises only a few verses in the book of Genesis; however it is full of a surprising content, theological and anthropological at the same time. The revelation and discovery of the nuptial meaning of the body explain man's original happiness and, at the same time, open the perspective of his earthly history, in which he will never avoid this indispensable "theme" of his own existence.

The following verses of the Book of Genesis, according to the Yahwist text of chapter 3, show, actually, that this "historical" perspective will be constructed differently from the beatifying "beginning" (after original sin). It is all the more necessary, however, to penetrate deeply into the mysterious structure, theological and at the same time anthropological, of this "beginning." In fact, in the whole perspective of his own "history," man will not fail to confer a nuptial meaning on his own body. Even if this meaning undergoes and will undergo many distortions, it will always remain the deepest level, which demands to be revealed in all its simplicity and purity, and to be shown in its whole truth, as a sign of the "image of God." The way that goes from the mystery of creation to the "redemption of the body" (cf. Rom. 8) also passes here.

Remaining, at present, on the threshold of this historical perspective, we clearly realize, on the basis of Genesis 2:23-25, the connection that exists between the revelation and the discovery of the nuptial meaning of the body and man's original happiness. This "nuptial" meaning is also beatifying and, as such, manifests in a word the whole reality of that donation of which the first pages of the Book of Genesis speak to us. Reading them, we are convinced of the fact that the awareness of the meaning of the body that is derived from them—in particular of its "nuptial" meaning—is the fundamental element of human existence in the world.

This "nuptial" meaning of the human body can be understood only in the context of the person. The body has a "nuptial" meaning because the man-person, as the Council says, is a creature that God willed for its own sake, and that, at the same time, can fully discover its true self only in a sincere giving of itself.

If Christ revealed to man and woman, over and above the vocation to marriage, another vocation—namely, that of renouncing marriage, in view of the kingdom of heaven—He highlighted, with this vocation, the same truth about the human person. If a man or a woman are capable of making a gift of themselves for the kingdom of heaven, this proves in its turn (and perhaps even more) that there is the freedom of the gift in the human body. It means that this body possesses a full "nuptial" meaning.

FOOTNOTES

1. "Furthermore, the Lord Jesus, when praying to the Father 'that they may all be one...even as we are one' (Jn. 17:21-22), has opened up new horizons closed to human reason by implying that there is a certain parallel between the union existing among the divine persons and the union of the sons of God in truth and love. It follows, then, that if man is the only creature on earth that God has willed for its own sake, man can fully discover his true self only in a sincere giving of himself" *(Gaudium et spes,* no. 24).

The strictly theological analysis of the Book of Genesis, in particular Gn. 2:23-25, allows us to refer to this text. This constitutes another step between "adequate anthropology" and "theology of the body," which is closely bound up with the discovery of the essential characteristics of personal existence in man's "theological prehistory." Although this may meet with opposition on the part of the evolutionist mentality (even among theologians), it would be difficult, however, not to realize that the text of the Book of Genesis that we have analyzed, especially Gn. 2:23-25, proves not only the "original," but also the "exemplary" dimension of the existence of man, in particular of man "as male and female."

2. Biblical tradition reports a distant echo of the physical perfection of the first man. The prophet Ezekiel, implicitly comparing the King of Tyre with Adam in Eden, writes as follows:

"You were the signet of perfection,
full of wisdom,
and perfect in beauty;
you were in Eden, the garden of God..."
(Ez. 28:12-13).

Mystery of Man's Original Innocence

General audience of January 30, 1980.

1. The reality of the gift and the act of giving, outlined in the first chapters of Genesis as the content constituting the mystery of creation, confirms that the radiation of love is an integral part of this same mystery. Only love creates the good, and it alone can, in a word, be perceived in all its dimensions and its aspects in created things and particularly in man. Its presence is almost the final result of that interpretation of the gift, which we are carrying out here. Original happiness, the beatifying "beginning" of man whom God created "male and female" (Gn. 1:27), the nuptial significance of the body in its original nakedness: all that expresses its radication in love.

This consistent giving, which goes back to the deepest roots of consciousness and sub-consciousness, to the ultimate levels of the subjective existence of both, man and woman, and which is reflected in their mutual "experience of the body," bears witness to its radication in love. The first verses of the Bible speak about it so much as to remove all doubt. They speak not only of the creation of the world and of man in the world, but also of grace, that is, of the communication of holiness, of the radiation of the Spirit, which produces a special state of "spiritualization" in that man, who in fact was the first. In biblical language, that is, in the language of Revelation, the adjective "first" means precisely "of God": "Adam, the son of God" (cf. Lk. 3:38).

2. Happiness is being rooted in love. Original happiness speaks to us of the "beginning" of man, who emerged from Love and initiated love. That happened in an irrevocable way, despite the subsequent sin and death. In His time, Christ will be a witness to this irreversible love of the Creator and Father, which had already been expressed in the mystery of creation and in the grace of original innocence. And therefore also the common "beginning" of man and woman, that is, the original truth of their body in masculinity and femininity, to which Genesis 2:25 draws our attention, does not know shame. This "beginning" can also be defined as the original and beatifying immunity from shame as the result of love.

FOUNDATION OF ORIGINAL INNOCENCE

3. This immunity directs us towards the mystery of man's original innocence. It is a mystery of his existence, prior to the knowledge of good and evil and almost "outside" it. The fact that man exists in this way, before the breaking of the first covenant with his Creator,

belongs to the fullness of the mystery of creation. If, as we have already said, creation is a gift to man, then his fullness and deepest dimension is determined by grace, that is, by participation in the interior life of God Himself, in His holiness. This is also, in man, the interior foundation and source of his original innocence. It is with this concept—and more precisely with that of "original justice"—that theology defines the state of man before original sin.

In the present analysis of the "beginning," which opens up for us the ways indispensable for understanding the theology of the body, we must dwell on the mystery of man's original state. Indeed, that very awareness of the body—rather, awareness of the meaning of the body—which we are trying to highlight through analysis of the "beginning," reveals the peculiarity of original innocence.

What is most manifested, perhaps, in Genesis 2:25, in a direct way, is precisely the mystery of this innocence, which the original man and woman both bear, each in himself or herself. The body itself is, in a way, an "eye" witness of this characteristic. It is significant that the affirmation contained in Genesis 2:25— about nakedness mutually free from shame—is a statement unique in its kind in the whole Bible, so that it will never be repeated. On the contrary, we can quote many texts in which nakedness will be connected with shame or even, in an even stronger sense, with "ignominy."[1]

DIMENSION OF GRACE

In this wide context the reasons are all the more visible for discovering in Genesis 2:25 a particular trace of the mystery of original innocence and a particular factor of its radiation in the human subject. This innocence belongs to the dimension of grace contained in the mystery of creation, that is, to that mysterious gift made to the inner man—to the human "heart" —which enables both of them, man and woman, to exist from the "beginning" in the mutual relationship of the disinterested gift of oneself.

In that is contained the revelation and at the same time the discovery of the "nuptial" meaning of the body in its masculinity and femininity. It can be understood why we speak, in this case, of revelation and at the same time of discovery. From the point of view of our analysis, it is essential that the discovery of the nuptial meaning of the body, which we read in the testimony of the Book of Genesis, takes place through original innocence; in fact, it is this discovery which reveals and highlights the latter.

ORIGINAL RIGHTEOUSNESS

4. Original innocence belongs to the mystery of man's "beginning," from which "historical" man was then separated by committing original sin. This does not mean, however, that he is not able to approach that

mystery by means of his theological knowledge. "Historical" man tries to understand the mystery of original innocence almost by means of a contrast, that is, going back also to the experience of his own sin and his own sinfulness.[2] He tries to understand original innocence as an essential characteristic for the theology of the body, starting from the experience of shame; in fact, the Bible text itself directs him in this way. Original innocence, therefore, is what "radically," that is, at its very roots, excludes shame of the body in the man-woman relationship, eliminates its necessity in man, in his heart, that is, in his conscience.

Although original innocence speaks above all of the Creator's gift, of the grace that made it possible for man to experience the meaning of the primary donation of the world, and in particular the meaning of the mutual donation of one to the other through masculinity and femininity in this world, this innocence, however, seems to refer above all to the interior state of the human "heart," of the human will. At least indirectly, there is included in it the revelation and discovery of human moral conscience, the revelation and discovery of the whole dimension of conscience—obviously, before the knowledge of good and evil. In a certain sense, it must be understood as original righteousness.

PURITY OF HEART

5. In the prism of our "historical *a posteriori*," we are trying, therefore, to reconstruct,

in a certain way, the characteristic of original innocence understood as the content of the reciprocal experience of the body as experience of its nuptial meaning (according to the testimony of Genesis 2:23-25). Since happiness and innocence are part of the framework of the communion of persons, as if it were a question of two convergent threads of man's existence in the very mystery of creation, the beatifying awareness of the meaning of the body—that is, of the nuptial meaning of human masculinity and femininity—is conditioned by original innocence.

It seems that there is no impediment to understanding that original innocence here as a particular "purity of heart," which preserves an interior faithfulness to the gift according to the nuptial meaning of the body. Consequently, original innocence, conceived in this way, is manifested as a tranquil testimony of conscience which (in this case) precedes any experience of good and evil; and yet this serene testimony of conscience is something all the more beatifying. It can be said, indeed, that awareness of the nuptial meaning of the body, in its masculinity and femininity, becomes "humanly" beatifying only by means of this testimony.

To this subject—that is, to the link which, in the analysis of man's "beginning," can be seen between his innocence (purity of heart) and his happiness—we shall devote the next meditation.

FOOTNOTES

1. "Nakedness," in the sense of "lack of clothing," in the ancient Middle East, meant the state of abjection of men deprived of freedom: slaves, prisoners of war or condemned persons, those who did not enjoy the protection of the law. In women, nakedness was considered a dishonor (cf., e.g., the threats of the prophets: Hosea 1:2 and Ezekiel 23:26, 29).

A free man, concerned about his dignity, had to be dressed sumptuously: The longer the trains of his clothes, the higher was his dignity (cf., e.g., Joseph's coat, which made his brothers jealous; or that of the Pharisees, who lengthened their fringes).

The second meaning of "nakedness," in the euphemistic sense, concerned the sexual act. The Hebrew word *cerwat* means a spatial emptiness (for example, of the landscape), lack of clothes, divesting, but there was in itself nothing disgraceful about it.

2. "We know that the law is spiritual; but I am carnal, sold under sin. I do not understand my own actions. For I do not do what I want but I do the very thing I hate.... So then it is no longer I that do it, but sin which dwells within me. For I know that nothing good dwells within me, that is, in my flesh. I can will what is right, but I cannot do it. For I do not do the good I want, but the evil I do not want is what I do. Now if I do what I do not want, it is no longer I that do it, but sin which dwells within me. So I find it to be a law that when I want to do right, evil lies close at hand. For I delight in the law of God, in my inmost self, but I see in my members another law at war with the law of my mind and making me captive to the law of sin which dwells in my members. Wretched man that I am! Who will deliver me from this body of death?" (Rom. 7:14-15, 17-24; cf. "*Video meliora proboque, deteriora sequor,*" Ovid, *Metamorph.* VII 20)

Man and Woman:
A Mutual Gift for Each Other

General audience of February 6, 1980.

1. Let us continue the examination of that "beginning," to which Jesus referred in His talk with the Pharisees on the subject of marriage. This reflection requires us to go beyond the threshold of man's history and arrive at the state of original innocence. To grasp the meaning of this innocence, we take as our basis, in a way, the experience of "historical" man, the testimony of his heart, of his conscience.

UNITED WITH INNOCENCE

2. Following the "historical *a posteriori*" line, let us try to reconstruct the peculiarity of original innocence enclosed within the mutual experience of the body and its nuptial meaning, according to Genesis 2:23-25. The situation described here reveals the beatifying experience of the meaning of the body which, within

the mystery of creation, man attains, so to speak, in the complementarity of what is male and female in him. However, at the root of this experience there must be the interior freedom of the gift, united above all with innocence. The human will is originally innocent and, in this way, the reciprocity and the exchange of the gift of the body, according to its masculinity and femininity, as the gift of the person, is facilitated. Consequently, the innocence to which Genesis 2:25 bears witness can be defined as innocence of the mutual experience of the body.

The sentence: "The man and his wife were both naked, and were not ashamed," expresses precisely this innocence in the reciprocal "experience of the body." It is an innocence which inspires the interior exchange of the gift of the person, which, in the mutual relationship, actualizes concretely the nuptial meaning of masculinity and femininity. In this way, therefore, to understand the innocence of the mutual experience of the body, we must try to clarify in what consists the interior innocence in the exchange of the gift of the person. This exchange constitutes, in fact, the real source of the experience of innocence.

RECIPROCAL ACCEPTANCE

3. We can say that interior innocence (that is, righteousness of intention) in the exchange

of the gift consists in reciprocal "acceptance" of the other, such as to correspond to the very essence of the gift; in this way, mutual donation creates the communion of persons. It is a question, therefore, of "receiving" the other human being and "accepting him," precisely because in this mutual relationship, of which Genesis 2:23-25 speaks, the man and the woman become a gift for each other, through the whole truth and evidence of their own body in its masculinity and femininity. It is a question, then, of an "acceptance" or "welcome" of such a kind that it expresses and sustains, in mutual nakedness, the meaning of the gift and, therefore, deepens the mutual dignity of it. This dignity corresponds profoundly to the fact that the Creator willed (and continually wills) man, male and female, "for his own sake." The innocence "of the heart," and consequently, the innocence of the experience, means a moral participation in the eternal and permanent act of God's will.

The opposite of this "welcoming" or "acceptance" of the other human being as a gift would be a privation of the gift itself and, therefore, a changing and even a reduction of the other to an "object for myself" (object of lust, of misappropriation, etc.).

We will not deal in detail now with this multiform, presumable antithesis of the gift. It is already necessary here, however, in the context of Genesis 2:23-25, to note that this extort-

ing of the gift from the other human being
(from the woman by the man and vice versa)
and reducing him (her) interiorly to a mere "object for me," should mark precisely the
beginning of shame. The latter, in fact, corresponds to a threat inflicted on the gift in its personal intimacy and bears witness to the interior
collapse of innocence in the mutual experience.

GIVING BECOMES ACCEPTING

4. According to Genesis 2:25, "the man
and his wife were not ashamed." This enables
us to reach the conclusion that the exchange of
the gift, in which the whole of their humanity,
body and soul, femininity and masculinity, participates, is actualized by preserving the interior characteristic (that is, precisely, innocence)
of the donation of oneself and of the acceptance
of the other as a gift. These two functions of
mutual exchange are deeply connected in the
whole process of the "gift of oneself": the giving
and the accepting of the gift interpenetrate, so
that the giving itself becomes accepting, and
the acceptance is transformed into giving.

REDISCOVERS HERSELF

5. Genesis 2:23-25 enables us to deduce
that woman who, in the mystery of creation,
"is given" to man by the Creator, is, thanks
to original innocence, "received," that is,

accepted by him as a gift. The Bible text is quite clear and limpid at this point. At the same time, the acceptance of the woman by the man and the very way of accepting her, become, as it were, a first donation, so that the woman, in giving herself (from the very first moment in which, in the mystery of creation, she was "given" to the man by the Creator), "rediscovers" at the same time "herself," thanks to the fact that she has been accepted and welcomed, and thanks to the way in which she has been received by the man.

So she finds herself again in the very fact of giving herself ("through a sincere gift of herself," cf. *Gaudium et spes*, no. 24), when she is accepted in the way in which the Creator wished her to be, that is, "for her own sake," through her humanity and femininity. When there is ensured in this acceptance the whole dignity of the gift, through the offer of what she is in the whole truth of her humanity and in the whole reality of her body and sex, of her femininity, she reaches the inner depth of her person and full possession of herself.

Let us add that this finding of oneself in giving oneself becomes the source of a new giving of oneself, which grows by virtue of the interior disposition to the exchange of the gift and to the extent to which it meets with the same and even deeper acceptance and welcome, as the fruit of a more and more intense awareness of the gift itself.

REAL COMMUNION OF PERSONS

6. It seems that the second narrative of creation has assigned to man "from the beginning" the function of the one who, above all, receives the gift (cf. particularly Genesis 2:23). "From the beginning" the woman is entrusted to his eyes, to his consciousness, to his sensitivity, to his "heart." He, on the other hand, must, in a way, ensure the same process of the exchange of the gift, the mutual interpenetration of giving and receiving as a gift, which, precisely through its reciprocity, creates a real communion of persons.

If the woman, in the mystery of creation, is the one who was "given" to the man, the latter, on his part, in receiving her as a gift in the full truth of her person and femininity, thereby enriches her, and at the same time he, too, in this mutual relationship, is enriched. The man is enriched not only through her, who gives him her own person and femininity, but also through the gift of himself. The man's giving of himself, in response to that of the woman, is an enrichment of himself. In fact, there is manifested in it, as it were, the specific essence of his masculinity which, through the reality of the body and of sex, reaches the deep recesses of the "possession of self," thanks to which he is capable both of giving himself and of receiving the other's gift.

The man, therefore, not only accepts the gift, but at the same time is received as a gift by the woman, in the revelation of the interior spiritual essence of his masculinity, together with the whole truth of his body and sex. Accepted in this way, he is enriched through this acceptance and welcoming of the gift of his own masculinity. Subsequently, this acceptance, in which the man finds himself again through the "sincere gift of himself," becomes in him the source of a new and deeper enrichment of the woman. The exchange is mutual, and in it the reciprocal effects of the "sincere gift" and of the "finding oneself again" are revealed and grow.

In this way, following the trail of the "historical *a posteriori*"—and above all, following the trail of human hearts—we can reproduce and, as it were, reconstruct that mutual exchange of the gift of the person, which was described in the ancient text, so rich and deep, of the Book of Genesis.

Original Innocence
and Man's Historical State

General audience of February 13, 1980.

1. Today's meditation presupposes what has already been established by the various analyses made up to now. They sprang from the answer given by Jesus to His interlocutors (Gospel of St. Matthew 19:3-9; and of St. Mark 10:1-12), who had asked Him a question about marriage, its indissolubility and unity. The Master had urged them to consider carefully that which was "from the beginning." Precisely for this reason, in the series of our meditations up to today, we have tried to reproduce somehow the reality of the union, or rather of the communion of persons, lived "from the beginning" by the man and the woman. Subsequently, we tried to penetrate into the content of verse 25 of Genesis 2, so concise: "And the man and his wife were both naked, and were not ashamed."

These words refer to the gift of original innocence, revealing its character synthetically, so to speak. Theology, on this basis, has constructed the global image of man's original innocence and justice, prior to original sin, by applying the method of objectivization, proper to metaphysics and metaphysical anthropology. In this analysis we are trying rather to take into consideration the aspect of human subjectivity; the latter, moreover, seems to be closer to the original texts, especially the second narrative of creation, that is, the Yahwist text.

2. Apart from a certain diversity of interpretation, it seems quite clear that "the experience of the body," such as it can be inferred from the ancient text of Genesis 2:23 and even more from Genesis 2:25, indicates a degree of "spiritualization" of man different from that of which the same text speaks after original sin (Gn. 3) and which we know from the experience of "historical" man. It is a different measure of "spiritualization," which involves another composition of the interior forces of man himself, almost another body-soul relationship, other inner proportions between sensitivity, spirituality and affectivity, that is, another degree of interior sensitiveness to the gifts of the Holy Spirit. All this conditions man's state of original innocence and at the same time determines it, permitting us also to understand the narrative of Genesis. Theology and also the Magisterium of the Church have given these fundamental truths a specific form.[1]

PERMANENT ROOTS OF "ETHOS" OF THE BODY

3. Undertaking the analysis of the "beginning" according to the dimension of the theology of the body, we do so on the basis of Christ's words in which He Himself referred to that "beginning." When He said: "Have you not read that he who made them from the beginning made them male and female?" (Mt. 19:4), He ordered us and He still orders us to return to the depths of the mystery of creation. We do so, fully aware of the gift of original innocence, characteristic of man before original sin. Although an insuperable barrier divides us from what man then was as male and female, by means of the gift of grace united with the mystery of creation, and from what they both were for each other, as a mutual gift, yet we try to understand that state of original innocence in its connection with man's "historical" state after original sin: "*status naturae lapsae simul et redemptae.*"

Through the category of the "historical *a posteriori*," we try to arrive at the original meaning of the body, and to grasp the connection existing between it and the nature of original innocence in the "experience of the body," as it is highlighted in such a significant way in the narrative of the Book of Genesis. We arrive at the conclusion that it is important and essential to define this connection, not only with regard to man's "theological prehistory," in which the life of the couple was almost completely permeated by the grace of original innocence, but also in relation to its possibility of revealing to us the permanent roots of the human and particularly the theological aspect of the ethos of the body.

ETHICALLY CONDITIONED

4. Man enters the world and, as it were, the most intimate pattern of his future and his history, with awareness of the nuptial meaning of his own body, of his own masculinity and femininity. Original innocence says that that meaning is conditioned "ethically," and furthermore that, on its part, it constitutes the future of the human *ethos*. This is very important for the theology of the body: it is the reason why we must construct this theology "from the beginning," carefully following the indication of Christ's words.

In the mystery of creation, man and woman were "given" in a special way to each other by the Creator, and that not only in the dimension of that first human couple and of that first communion of persons, but in the whole perspective of the existence of mankind and of the human family. The fundamental fact of this existence of man at every stage of his history is that God "created them male and female"; in fact, He always creates them in this way and they are always such. Understanding of the fundamental meanings, contained in the very mystery of creation, such as the nuptial meaning of the body (and of the fundamental conditionings of this meaning), is important and indispensable in order to know who man is and who he should be, and therefore how he should mold his own activity. It is an essential and important thing for the future of the human *ethos*.

5. Genesis 2:24 notes that the two, man and woman, were created for marriage: "Therefore, a man leaves his father and his mother and cleaves to his wife, and they become one flesh." In this way a great creative perspective is opened: precisely the perspective of man's existence, which is continually renewed by means of "procreation" (we could say "self-reproduction").

This perspective is deeply rooted in the consciousness of humanity (cf. Gn. 2:23) and also in the particular consciousness of the nuptial meaning of the body (Gn. 2:25). The man and the woman, before becoming husband and wife (later Gn. 4:1 speaks of this in the concrete), emerge from the mystery of creation in the first place as brother and sister in the same humanity. Understanding of the nuptial meaning of the body in its masculinity and femininity reveals the depths of their freedom, which is freedom of giving.

From here there begins that communion of persons, in which both meet and give themselves to each other in the fullness of their subjectivity. Thus both grow as persons-subjects, and they grow mutually one for the other also

through their body and through that "nakedness" free of shame. In this communion of persons the whole depth of the original solitude of
man (of the first one and of all) is perfectly
ensured and, at the same time, this solitude
becomes in a marvelous way permeated and
broadened by the gift of the "other." If the man
and the woman cease to be a disinterested gift
for each other, as they were in the mystery of
creation, then they recognize that "they are
naked" (cf. Gn. 3). And then the shame of that
nakedness, which they had not felt in the state
of original innocence, will spring up in their
hearts.

Original innocence manifests and at the
same time constitutes the perfect *ethos* of the
gift.

We will return to this subject again.

FOOTNOTES

1. "If one should not acknowledge that the first man
Adam, on transgressing God's command in paradise, did
not immediately lose the holiness and justice in which he
had been constituted...let him be anathema" (Council of
Trent, Sess. V, con. 1, 2; D.B. 788, 789).

"The first parents had been constituted in a state of
holiness and justice (...). The state of original justice conferred on the first parents was gratuitous and truly super-
natural (...). The first parents were constituted in a state
of integral nature, i.e., immune from concupiscence,
ignorance, pain and death...and they enjoyed a unique happiness (...). The gifts of integrity granted to the first parents
were gratuitous and preternatural" (A. Tanquerey, *Synop-
sis Theologiae Dogmaticae*, Paris, 1943,[24] pp. 543-549).

Man Enters the World
a Subject of Truth and Love

General audience of February 20, 1980.

1. The Book of Genesis points out that man and woman were created for marriage: "...a man leaves his father and his mother and cleaves to his wife, and they become one flesh" (Gn. 2:24). In this way there opens the great creative perspective of human existence, which is always renewed by means of "procreation" which is "self-reproduction." This perspective is rooted in the consciousness of mankind and also in the particular understanding of the nuptial meaning of the body, with its masculinity and femininity. Man and woman, in the mystery of creation, are a mutual gift. Original innocence manifests and at the same time determines the perfect ethos of the gift.

We spoke about that at the preceding meeting. Through the ethos of the gift the problem of the "subjectivity" of man, who is a subject made in the image and likeness of God, is partly outlined. In the narrative of creation (particularly in Gn. 2:23-25) "the woman" is certainly not merely "an object" for the man, though they both remain in front of each other in all the fullness of their objectivity as creatures, as "bone of my bones and flesh of my flesh," as male and female, both naked. Only the nakedness that makes woman an "object" for man, or vice versa, is a source of shame. The fact that "they were not ashamed" means that the woman was not an "object" for the man nor he for her.

Interior innocence as "purity of heart" made it impossible somehow for one to be reduced by the other to the level of a mere object. The fact that they "were not ashamed" means that they were united by awareness of the gift; they were mutually conscious of the nuptial meaning of their bodies, in which the freedom of the gift is expressed and all the interior riches of the person as subject are manifested.

This mutual interpenetration of the "self" of the human persons, of the man and of the woman, seems to exclude subjectively any "reduction to an object." In this is revealed the subjective profile of that love of which it can be said, on the other hand, that "it is objective" to the depths, since it is nourished by the mutual "objectivity" of the gift.

2. After original sin, man and woman will lose the grace of original innocence. The discovery of the nuptial meaning of the body will cease to be for them a simple reality of revelation and grace. However, this meaning

will remain as a commitment given to man by the ethos of the gift, inscribed in the depths of the human heart, as a distant echo of original innocence. From that nuptial meaning human love in its interior truth and its subjective authenticity will be formed. And man—also through the veil of shame—will continually rediscover himself as the guardian of the mystery of the subject, that is, of the freedom of the gift, so as to defend it from any reduction to the position of a mere object.

3. For the present, however, we are before the threshold of man's earthly history. The man and the woman have not yet crossed it towards knowledge of good and evil. They are immersed in the mystery of creation; and the depth of this mystery hidden in their hearts is innocence, grace, love and justice: "And God saw everything that he had made, and behold, it was very good" (Gn. 1:31).

Man appears in the visible world as the highest expression of the divine gift, because he bears within him the interior dimension of the gift. And with it he brings into the world his particular likeness to God, with which he transcends and dominates also his "visibility" in the world, his corporality, his masculinity or femininity, his nakedness. A reflection of this likeness is also the primordial awareness of the nuptial meaning of the body, pervaded by the mystery of original innocence.

4. Thus, in this dimension, there is constituted a primordial sacrament, understood as

a sign that transmits effectively in the visible world the invisible mystery hidden in God from time immemorial. And this is the mystery of truth and love, the mystery of divine life, in which man really participates. In the history of man, it is original innocence which begins this participation and it is also a source of original happiness. The sacrament, as a visible sign, is constituted with man, as a "body," by means of his "visible" masculinity and femininity. The body, in fact, and it alone, is capable of making visible what is invisible: the spiritual and the divine. It was created to transfer into the visible reality of the world the mystery hidden since time immemorial in God, and thus be a sign of it.

5. So in man created in the image of God there was revealed, in a way, the very sacramentality of creation, the sacramentality of the world. Man, in fact, by means of his corporality, his masculinity and femininity, becomes a visible sign of the economy of truth and love, which has its source in God Himself and which was revealed already in the mystery of creation. Against this vast background we understand fully the words that constitute the sacrament of marriage, present in Genesis 2:24 ("A man leaves his father and his mother and cleaves to his wife, and they become one flesh").

Against this vast background, we understand, furthermore, that the words of Genesis 2:25 ("they were both naked, and were not ashamed"), through the whole depth of their anthropological meaning, express the fact that, together with man, holiness entered the visible world, created for him. The sacrament of the world, and the sacrament of man in the world, comes from the divine source of holiness, and at the same time is instituted for holiness. Original innocence, connected with the experience of the nuptial meaning of the body, is the same holiness that enables man to express himself deeply with his own body, and that, precisely, by means of the "sincere gift" of himself. Awareness of the gift conditions, in this case, "the sacrament of the body": in his body as male or female, man feels he is a subject of holiness.

6. With this consciousness of the meaning of his own body, man, as male and female, enters the world as a subject of truth and love. It can be said that Genesis 2:23-25 narrates, as it were, the first feast of humanity in all the original fullness of the experience of the nuptial meaning of the body. It is a feast of humanity, which draws its origin from the divine sources of truth and love in the very mystery of creation. And although, very soon, the horizon of sin and death is extended over that original feast (Gn. 3), yet right from the mystery of creation we already draw a first hope: that is, that the fruit of the divine economy of truth and love, which was revealed "at the beginning," is not death, but life, and not so much the destruction of the body of the man created "in the image of God," as rather the "call to glory" (cf. Rom. 8:30).

Analysis of Knowledge
and of Procreation

General audience of March 5, 1980.

1. To the ensemble of our analyses, dedicated to the biblical "beginning," we wish to add another short passage, taken from chapter 4 of the Book of Genesis. For this purpose, however, it is always necessary to refer first of all to the words spoken by Jesus Christ in the talk with the Pharisees (cf. Mt. 19 and Mk. 10),[1] in the compass of which our reflections take place. They concern the context of human existence, according to which death and the destruction of the body connected with it (according to the words: "to dust you shall return" of Gn. 3:19) have become the common fate of man. Christ refers to "the beginning," to the original dimension of the mystery of creation, when this dimension had already been shattered by the *mysterium iniquitatis*, that is, by sin and, together with it, also by death: *mysterium mortis.*

Sin and death entered man's history, in a way, through the very heart of that unity which, from "the beginning," was formed by man and woman, created and called to become "one flesh" (Gn. 2:24). Already at the beginning of our meditations we saw that Christ, referring to "the beginning," leads us, in a certain way, beyond the limit of man's hereditary sinfulness to his original innocence. He enables us, in this way, to find the continuity and the connection existing between these two situations, by means of which the drama of the origins was produced as well as the revelation of the mystery of man to historical man.

This, so to speak, authorizes us to pass, after the analyses concerning the state of original innocence, to the last of them, that is, to the analysis of "knowledge and of procreation." Thematically, it is closely bound up with the blessing of fertility, which is inserted in the first narrative of man's creation as male and female (Gn. 1:27-28). Historically, on the other hand, it is already inserted in that horizon of sin and death which, as the Book of Genesis teaches (Gn. 3), has weighed on the consciousness of the meaning of the human body, together with the breaking of the first covenant with the Creator.

UNION DEFINED AS KNOWLEDGE

2. In Genesis 4, and therefore still within the scope of the Yahwist text, we read: "Adam knew Eve his wife, and she conceived and bore Cain, saying, 'I have gotten a man with the help of the Lord.' And again, she bore his brother Abel" (Gn. 4:1-2). If we connect with "knowl-

edge" that first fact of the birth of a man on earth, we do so on the basis of the literal translation of the text, according to which the conjugal "union" is defined as "knowledge": "Adam *knew* Eve his wife," a translation of the Semitic term *jādāc*.[2]

We can see in this a sign of the poverty of the archaic language, which lacked varied expressions to define differentiated facts. Nevertheless, it is significant that the situation, in which husband and wife unite so closely as to become "one flesh," has been defined as "knowledge." In this way, in fact, from the very poverty of the language there seems to emerge a specific depth of meaning, which derives, precisely, from all the meanings hitherto analyzed.

BECOMING ONE

3. Evidently, this is also important as regards the "archetype" of our way of conceiving corporeal man, his masculinity and his femininity, and therefore his sex. In this way, in fact, through the term "knowledge" used in Genesis 4:1-2 and often in the Bible, the conjugal relationship of man and woman, that is, the fact that they become, through the duality of sex, "one flesh," was raised and introduced into the specific dimension of persons. Genesis 4:1-2 speaks only of "knowledge" of the woman by the man, as if to stress above all the activity of the latter. It is also possible, however, to speak of the reciprocity of this "knowledge," in which

man and woman participate by means of their body and their sex. Let us add that a series of subsequent biblical texts, as, moreover, the same chapter of Genesis (cf., for example, Gn. 4:17; 4:25), speak with the same language. And so up to the words spoken by Mary of Nazareth in the annunciation: "How shall this be, since I know not man?" (Lk. 1:34)

DEEPEST REALITY

4. Thus, with that biblical "knew," which appears for the first time in Genesis 4:1-2, we find ourselves in the presence of, on the one hand, the direct expression of human intentionality (because it is characteristic of knowledge) and, on the other, of the whole reality of conjugal life and union, in which man and woman become "one flesh."

Speaking here of "knowledge," even though due to the poverty of the language, the Bible indicates the deepest essence of the reality of married life. This essence appears as an element and at the same time a result of those meanings, the trace of which we have been trying to follow from the beginning of our study; it is part, in fact, of the awareness of the meaning of one's own body. In Genesis 4:1, becoming "one flesh," the man and the woman experience in a particular way the meaning of their body. Together they become, in this way, almost the one subject of that act and that experience, while remaining, in this unity, two really different subjects. In a way, this authorizes the statement that "the husband knows his wife" or that both "know" each other. Then they reveal themselves to each other, with that specific depth of their own human "self," which, precisely, is revealed also by means of their sex, their masculinity and femininity. And then, in a unique way, the woman "is given" to the man to be known, and he to her.

UNIQUENESS OF PERSON

5. If we are to maintain continuity with regard to the analyses made up to the present (particularly the last ones, which interpret man in the dimension of a gift), it should be pointed out that, according to the Book of Genesis, *datum* and *donum* are equivalent.

However, Genesis 4:1-2 stresses above all *datum*. In conjugal "knowledge," the woman "is given" to the man and he to her, since the body and sex directly enter the structure and the very content of this "knowledge." In this way, therefore, the reality of the conjugal union, in which the man and the woman become "one flesh," contains a new and, in a way, definitive discovery of the meaning of the human body in its masculinity and femininity. But, in connection with this discovery, is it right to speak only of "sexual life together"? It is necessary to take into consideration that each of them, man and woman, is not just a passive object, defined by his or her own body and sex, and in this way determined "by nature." On the contrary, precisely because of the fact that they are a man and a woman, each of them is "given" to the other as a unique and unrepeatable subject, as "self," as a person.

Sex decides not only the somatic individuality of man, but defines at the same time his personal identity and concreteness. Precisely in this personal identity and concreteness, as an unrepeatable female-male "self," man is "known" when the words of Genesis 2:24 come true: "A man...cleaves to his wife, and they become one flesh." The "knowledge," of which Genesis 4:1-2 and all the following biblical texts speak, arrives at the deepest roots of this identity and concreteness, which man and woman owe to their sex. This concreteness means both the uniqueness and the unrepeatability of the person.

It was worthwhile, therefore, to reflect on the eloquence of the biblical text quoted and of the word "knew." In spite of the apparent lack of terminological precision, it allows us to dwell on the depth and dimension of a concept, of which our contemporary language, very precise though it is, often deprives us.

FOOTNOTES

1. The fact must be kept in mind that, in the talk with the Pharisees (Mt. 19:7-9; Mk. 10:4-6), Christ takes up a position with regard to the practice of the Mosaic law concerning the so-called "certificate of divorce." The words: "for your hardness of heart," spoken by Christ, reflect not only "the history of hearts," but also the whole complexity of the positive law of the Old Testament, which always sought a "human compromise" in this delicate field.

2. "To know" (jādāc) in biblical language does not mean only a purely intellectual knowledge, but also concrete knowledge, such as, for example, the experience of suffering (cf. Is. 53:3), of sin (Wis. 3:13), of war and peace (Jgs. 3:1; Is. 59:8). From this experience there also springs moral judgment: "knowledge of good and evil" (Gn. 2:9-17).

"Knowledge" enters the field of interpersonal relations when it regards family solidarity (Dt. 33:9) and especially conjugal relations. Precisely in reference to the conjugal act, the term stresses the paternity of illustrious characters and the origin of their offspring (cf. Gn. 4:1, 25; 4:17; 1 Sm. 1:19), as valid data for genealogy, to which the tradition of priests (hereditary in Israel) attached great importance.

"Knowledge," however, could also mean all other sexual relations, even illicit ones (cf. Nm. 31:17; Gn. 19:5; Jgs. 19:22).

In the negative form, the verb denotes abstention from sexual relations, especially if it is a question of virgins (cf., for example, 1 Kgs. 2:4; Jgs. 11:39). In this field, the New Testament uses two Hebraisms, speaking of Joseph (Mt. 1:25) and of Mary (Lk. 1:34).

The aspect of the existential relationship of "knowledge" takes on a special meaning when its subject or object is God Himself (for example, Ps. 139; Jer. 31:34; Hos. 2:22; and also Jn. 14:7-9; 17:3).

Mystery of Woman Revealed in Motherhood

General audience of March 12, 1980.

1. In the preceding meditation, we analyzed the sentence of Genesis 4:1 and, in particular, the term "knew," used in the original text to define conjugal union. We also pointed out that this biblical "knowledge" establishes a kind of personal archetype[1] of corporality and human sexuality. That seems absolutely fundamental in order to understand man, who, from the "beginning," is in search of the meaning of his own body. This meaning is at the basis of the theology of the body itself. The term "knew" (Gn. 4:1-2) synthesizes the whole density of the biblical text analyzed so far.

The "man" who, according to Genesis 4:1, "knows" the woman, his wife, for the first time in the act of conjugal union, is, in fact, that same man who, by imposing names, that is also by "knowing," "differentiated himself" from the whole world of living beings or *animalia*, affirming himself as a person and subject. The "knowledge," of which Genesis 4:1 speaks, does not and cannot take him away from the level of that original and fundamental self-awareness. So—whatever a one-sidedly "naturalistic" mentality might say about it—in Genesis 4:1 it cannot be a question of passive acceptance of one's own determination by the body and by sex, precisely because it is a question of "knowledge"!

It is, on the contrary, a further discovery of the meaning of one's own body, a common and reciprocal discovery, just as the existence of man, whom "God created male and female," is common and reciprocal from the beginning. Knowledge, which was at the basis of man's original solitude, is now at the basis of this unity of the man and the woman, the clear perspective of which was enclosed by the Creator in the very mystery of creation (Gn. 1:27; 2:23). In this "knowledge," man confirms the meaning of the name "Eve," given to his wife, "because she was the mother of all living" (Gn. 3:20).

MYSTERY OF FEMININITY REVEALED

2. According to Genesis 4:1, the one who knows is the man, and the one who is known is the woman-wife, as if the specific determination of the woman, through her own body and sex, hid what constitutes the very depth of her femininity. The man, on the other hand, is the one who—after the sin—was the first to feel the

shame of his nakedness, and was the first to say: "I was afraid, because I was naked; and I hid myself" (Gn. 3:10). It will be necessary further to return separately to the state of mind of them both after the loss of original innocence.

Straightway, however, it should be noted that in the "knowledge," of which Genesis 4:1 speaks, the mystery of femininity is manifested and revealed completely by means of motherhood, as the text says: "she conceived and bore...." The woman stands before the man as a mother, the subject of the new human life that is conceived and develops in her, and from her is born into the world. Likewise, the mystery of man's masculinity, that is, the generative and "fatherly" meaning of his body, is also thoroughly revealed.[2]

BY MEANS OF THE BODY

3. The theology of the body, contained in the Book of Genesis, is concise and sparing of words. At the same time, fundamental contents, in a certain sense primary and definitive, find expression in it. Everyone finds himself again in his own way, in that biblical "knowledge." The constitution of the woman is different, as compared with the man; we know, in fact, today that it is different even in the deepest bio-physiological determinants. It is manifested externally only to a certain extent, in the construction and form of her body. Maternity manifests this constitution internally, as the particular potentiality of the female organism,

which with creative peculiarity serves for the conception and begetting of the human being, with the help of man. "Knowledge" conditions begetting.

Begetting is a perspective, which man and woman insert in their mutual "knowledge." The latter, therefore, goes beyond the limits of subject-object, such as man and woman seem to be mutually, since "knowledge" indicates on the one side him who "knows" and on the other side her who "is known" (or vice versa). In this "knowledge" is enclosed also the consummation of marriage, the specific *consummatum*; in this way the reaching of the "objectivity" of the body, hidden in the somatic potentialities of the man and of the woman, is obtained, and at the same time the reaching of the objectivity of the man who "is" this body. By means of the body, the human person is "husband" and "wife"; at the same time, in this particular act of "knowledge," mediated by personal femininity and masculinity, also the discovery of the "pure" subjectivity of the gift—that is, mutual self-fulfillment in the gift—seems to be reached.

THEIR LIVING IMAGE

4. Procreation brings it about that "the man and the woman (his wife)" know each other reciprocally in the "third," sprung from them both. Therefore, this "knowledge" becomes a discovery, in a way a revelation of the new man, in whom both of them, man and woman, again recognize themselves, their humanity, their liv-

ing image. In everything that is determined by both of them through the body and sex, "knowledge" inscribes a living and real content. So "knowledge" in the biblical sense means that the "biological" determination of man, by his body and sex, stops being something passive, and reaches the specific level and content of self-conscious and self-determinant persons. Therefore, it involves a particular consciousness of the meaning of the human body, bound up with fatherhood and motherhood.

EULOGY OF MOTHERHOOD

5. The whole exterior constitution of woman's body, its particular aspect, the qualities which, with the power of perennial attractiveness, are at the beginning of the "knowledge," of which Genesis 4:1-2 speaks ("Adam knew Eve his wife"), are in close union with motherhood. The Bible (and subsequently the liturgy), with its characteristic simplicity, honors and praises throughout the centuries "the womb that bore you and the breasts that you sucked" (Lk. 11:27). These words constitute a eulogy of motherhood, of femininity, of the female body in its typical expression of creative love. And they are words referred in the Gospel to the Mother of Christ, Mary, the second Eve. The first woman, on the other hand, at the moment when the maternal maturity of her body was revealed for the first time, when "she conceived and bore," said: "I have gotten a man with the help of the Lord" (Gn. 4:1).

WOMAN FULLY AWARE

6. These words express the whole theological depth of the function of begetting-procreating. The woman's body becomes the place of the conception of the new man.[3] In her womb, the conceived man assumes his specific human aspect, before being born. The somatic homogeneousness of man and woman, which found its first expression in the words: "This is bone of my bones and flesh of my flesh" (Gn. 2:23), is confirmed in turn by the words of the first woman-mother: "I have gotten a man!" The first woman, giving birth, is fully aware of the mystery of creation, which is renewed in human generation. She is also fully aware of the creative participation that God has in human generation, His work and that of her husband, since she says: "I have gotten a man with the help of the Lord."

There cannot be any confusion between the spheres of action of the causes. The first parents transmit to all human parents—even after sin, together with the fruit of the tree of knowledge of good and evil and almost at the threshold of all "historical" experiences—the fundamental truth about the birth of man in the image of God, according to natural laws. In this new man—born of the woman-parent thanks to the man-parent—there is reproduced every time the very "image of God," of that God who constituted the humanity of the first man: "God created man in his own image; male and female he created them" (Gn. 1:27).

WITH THE LORD'S HELP

7. Although there are deep differences between man's state of original innocence and his state of hereditary sinfulness, that "image of God" constitutes a basis of continuity and unity. The "knowledge," of which Genesis 4:1 speaks, is the act which originates being, or rather, which in union with the Creator, establishes a new man in his existence. The first man, in his transcendental solitude, took possession of the visible world, created for him, knowing and imposing names on living beings (animalia). The same "man," as male and female, knowing each other in this specific community-communion of persons, in which the man and woman are united so closely with each other as to become "one flesh," constitutes humanity, that is, confirms and renews the existence of man as the image of God. Every time both of them, man and woman, take up again, so to speak, this image from the mystery of creation and transmit it "with the help of the Lord God."

The words of the Book of Genesis, which are a testimony of the first birth of man on earth, enclose within them at the same time everything that can and must be said of the dignity of human generation.

FOOTNOTES

1. As for archetypes, C.G. Jung describes them as "a priori" forms of various functions of the soul: perception of relations, creative fantasy. The forms fill up with content with materials of experience. They are not inert, but are

charged with sentiment and tendency (see particularly: "Die psychologischen Aspekte des Mutterarchetypus," Eranos 6, 1938, pp. 405-409).

According to this conception, an archetype can be met with in the mutual man-woman relationship, a relationship which is based on the dual and complementary realization of the human being in two sexes. The archetype will fill up with content by means of individual and collective experience, and can trigger off fantasy, the creator of images. It would be necessary to specify that the archetype: a) is not limited to, or exalted in, physical intercourse, but includes the relationship of "knowing"; b) it is charged with tendency: desire-fear, gift-possession; c) the archetype, as proto-image ("Urbild"), is a generator of images ("Bilder").

The third aspect enables us to pass to hermeneutics, in the concrete, that of texts of Scripture and of Tradition. Primary religious language is symbolic (cf. W. Stählin, *Symbolon*, 1958; I. Macquarrie, *God Talk*, 1968; T. Fawcett, *The Symbolic Language of Religion*, 1970). Among the symbols, he prefers some radical or exemplary ones, which we can call archetypal. Well, among them the Bible uses the symbol of the conjugal relationship, concretely at the level of the "knowing" described.

One of the first poems of the Bible, which applies the conjugal archetype to God's relations with His people, culminates in the verb commented on: "You shall know the Lord" (Hos. 2:22: we yadacta 'et Yhwh; weakened to "You will know that I am the Lord = *wydct ky 'ny Yhwh:* Is. 49:23; 60:16; Ez. 16:62, which are the three "conjugal" poems). A literary tradition starts from here, which will culminate in the Pauline application of Ephesians 5 to Christ and to the Church; then it will pass to patristic tradition and to that of the great mystics (for example, "Llama de amor viva" of St. John of the Cross).

In the treatise "Grundzüge der Literatur—und Sprachwissenschaft," vol. I, München 1976, 4 ed., p. 462, archetypes are defined as follows: "Archaic images and motifs which, according to Jung, form the content of the collective unconscious common to all men; they present symbols, which, in all times and among all peoples, bring to life in a figurative way what is decisive for humanity as regards ideas, representations and instincts."

Freud, it seems, does not use the concept of archetype. He establishes a symbolism or code of fixed correspondences between present-patent images and latent thoughts. The meaning of the symbols is fixed, even if not just one; they may be reducible to an ultimate thought that is irreducible, which is usually some experience of childhood. These are primary and of sexual character (but he does not call them archetypes). See T. Todorov, *Théories du symbole*, Paris, 1977, pp. 317f.; also: J. Jacoby, *Komplex, Archetyp, Symbol in der Psychologie C.G. Jung*, Zurich 1957.

2. Fatherhood is one of the most important aspects of humanity in Holy Scripture.

The text of Genesis 5:3: "Adam...became the father of a son *in his own likeness, after his image*" is explicitly linked up with the narrative of the creation of man (Gn. 1:27; 5:1) and seems to attribute to the earthly father participation in the divine work of transmitting life, and perhaps also in that joy present in the affirmation: (God) "saw everything that he had made, and behold, it was very good" (Gn. 1:31).

3. According to the text of Gn. 1:26, the "call" to existence is at the same time the transmission of the divine image and likeness. Man must proceed to transmit this image, thus continuing God's work. The narrative of the generation of Seth stresses this aspect: "When Adam had lived a hundred and thirty years, he became the father of a son in his own likeness, after his image" (Gn. 5:3). Since Adam and Eve were the image of God, Seth inherits this likeness from his parents to transmit it to others.

In Holy Scripture, however, every vocation is united with a mission; so the call to existence is already a predestination to God's work: "Before I formed you in the womb I knew you, and before you were born I consecrated you" (Jer. 1:5; cf. also Is. 44:1; 9:1-5).

God is the One who not only calls to existence, but sustains and develops life from the first moment of conception: "Yet you are he who took me from the womb; you kept me safe upon my mother's breasts. Upon you was I cast from my birth, and since my mother bore me you have been my God" (Ps. 22:10, 11; cf. Ps. 139:13-15).

The attention of the biblical author is focused on *the very fact* of the gift of life. Interest in the way in which this takes place is rather secondary and appears only in the later books (cf. Jb. 10:8, 11; 2 Mc. 7:22-23; Wis. 7:1-3).

Knowledge-Generation Cycle and Perspective of Death

General audience, March 26, 1980.

1. We are drawing to the end of the cycle of reflections wherein we have tried to follow Christ's appeal handed down to us by Matthew (19:3-9) and by Mark (10:1-12): "Have you not read that he who made them from the beginning made them male and female, and said, 'For this reason a man shall leave his father and mother and be joined to his wife, and the two shall become one flesh?' " (Mt. 19:4-5) Conjugal union, in the Book of Genesis, is defined as "knowledge": "Adam knew Eve his wife, and she conceived and bore...saying, 'I have gotten a man with the help of the Lord' " (Gn. 4:1). We have tried already, in our preceding meditations, to throw light on the content of that biblical "knowledge." With it man, male-female, not only gives his own name, as he did when he gave names to the other living beings *(animalia)*, thus taking possession of them, but "knows" in the sense of Genesis 4:1 (and other

passages of the Bible), that is, *realizes* what the name "man" expresses: realizes humanity in the new man generated. In a sense, therefore, he realizes himself, that is, the man-person.

2. In this way, the biblical cycle of "knowledge-generation" closes. This cycle of "knowledge" is constituted by the union of persons in love, which enables them to unite so closely that they become one flesh. The Book of Genesis reveals to us fully the truth of this cycle. Man, male and female, who, by means of the "knowledge" of which the Bible speaks, conceives and generates a new being, like himself, to whom he can give the name of "man" ("I have gotten a man"), takes possession, so to speak, of his humanity, or rather retakes possession of it. However, that happens in a different way from the manner in which he had taken possession of all other living beings *(animalia)* when he had given them their names. In fact, on that occasion, he had become their master, he had begun to carry out the content of the Creator's mandate: "Subdue the earth and have dominion over it" (cf. Gn. 1:28).

3. The first part, however, of the same command: "Be fruitful and multiply, and fill the earth" (Gn. 1:28), conceals another content and indicates another element. The man and the woman, in this "knowledge," in which they give rise to a being similar to them—of which they can say that "this is bone of my bones and flesh of my flesh" (Gn. 2:24)—are almost "carried off" together, are both taken possession of

by the humanity which they, in union and in mutual "knowledge," wish to express again, take possession of again, deriving it from themselves, from their own humanity, from the marvelous male and female maturity of their bodies and finally—through the whole sequence of human conceptions and generations right from the beginning—from the very mystery of creation.

4. In this sense, biblical "knowledge" can be explained as "possession." Is it possible to see in it some biblical equivalent of *eros*? It is a question here of two conceptual spheres, of two languages: biblical and Platonic; only with great caution can they be used to interpret each other.[1] It seems, however, that in the original revelation the idea of man's possession of the woman, or vice versa, as of an object, is not present. On the other hand, it is well known that as a result of the sinfulness contracted after original sin, man and woman must reconstruct, with great effort, the meaning of the disinterested mutual gift. This will be the subject of our further analyses.

5. The revelation of the body, contained in the Book of Genesis, particularly in chapter 3, shows with impressive clearness that the cycle of "knowledge-generation," so deeply rooted in the potentiality of the human body, was subjected, after sin, to the law of suffering and death. God-Yahweh says to the woman: "I will greatly multiply your pain in childbearing; in

pain you shall bring forth children" (Gn. 3:16). The horizon of death opens up before man, together with revelation of the generative meaning of the body in the spouses' act of mutual "knowledge." And lo, the first man, male, gives his wife the name Eve, "because she was the mother of all living" (Gn. 3:20), when he had already heard the words of the sentence which determined the whole perspective of human existence "within" the knowledge of good and evil. This perspective is confirmed by the words: "...you shall return to the ground, for out of it you were taken; you are dust, and to dust you shall return" (Gn. 3:19).

The radical character of this sentence is confirmed by the evidence of the experiences of man's whole earthly history. The horizon of death extends over the whole perspective of human life on earth, life that was inserted in that original biblical cycle of "knowledge-generation." Man, who has broken the covenant with his Creator by picking the fruit of the tree of the knowledge of good and evil, is detached by God-Yahweh from the tree of life: "Now, let him not put forth his hand and take also of the tree of life, and eat, and live for ever" (Gn. 3:21). In this way, the life given to man in the mystery of creation has not been taken away, but restricted by the limit of conceptions, births and death, and further aggravated by the perspective of hereditary sinfulness; but it is given to him again, in a way, as a task in the same ever-recurring cycle.

The sentence: "Adam knew his wife, and she conceived and bore..." (Gn. 4:1) is, as it were, a seal impressed on the original revelation of the body at the very "beginning" of man's history on earth. This history is always formed anew in its most fundamental dimension as if from the "beginning," by means of the same "knowledge-generation" of which the Book of Genesis speaks.

6. Thus, each man bears within him the mystery of his "beginning" closely bound up with awareness of the generative meaning of the body. Genesis 4:1-2 seems to be silent on the subject of the relationship between the generative and the nuptial meaning of the body. Perhaps it is not yet the time or the place to clarify this relationship, even though it seems indispensable in the further analysis. It will be necessary, then, to raise again the questions connected with the appearance of shame in man, shame of his masculinity and femininity, not experienced before. At this moment, however, this is in the background.

In the foreground there remains, however, the fact that "Adam knew Eve his wife, and she conceived and bore...." This is precisely the threshold of man's history. It is his "beginning" on the earth. On this threshold man, as male and female, stands with the awareness of the generative meaning of his own body: masculinity conceals within it the meaning of fatherhood, and femininity that of motherhood. In the name of this meaning, Christ will one day give the categorical answer to the question that the Pharisees had asked Him (Mt. 19; Mk. 10). We, on the other hand, penetrating the simple content of this answer, are trying at the same time to shed light on the context of that "beginning" to which Christ referred. The theology of the body has its roots in it.

7. Awareness of the meaning of the body and awareness of its generative meaning come into contact, in man, with awareness of death, the inevitable horizon of which they bear within them, so to speak. Yet there always returns in the history of man the "knowledge-generation" cycle, in which life struggles, ever anew, with the inexorable perspective of death, and always overcomes it. It is as if the reason for this refusal of life to surrender, which is manifested in "generation," were always the same "knowledge," with which man goes beyond the solitude of his own being, and, in fact, decides again to affirm this being in an "other." Both of them, man and woman, affirm it in the new man generated.

In this affirmation, biblical "knowledge" seems to acquire an even greater dimension. It seems to take its place in that "vision" of God Himself, with which there ends the first narrative of the creation of man about the "male" and the "female" made "in the image of God": God saw everything that He had made and...it was very good (Gn. 1:31). Man, in spite of all the experiences of his life, in spite of suffering, disappointment with himself, his sinfulness, and, finally, in spite of the inevitable prospect of death, always continues, however, to put "knowledge" at the "beginning" of "generation." In this way, he seems to participate in that first "vision" of God Himself: God the Creator "saw..., and behold, it was very good." And, ever anew, He confirms the truth of these words.

FOOTNOTES

1. According to Plato, *eros* is love athirst for transcendent Beauty and expresses insatiability straining towards its eternal object; therefore, it always raises what is human towards the divine, which alone is able to satisfy the nostalgia of the soul imprisoned in matter. It is a love that does not draw back before the greatest effort, in order to reach the ecstasy of union; therefore, it is an egocentric love, it is lust, although directed to sublime values (cf. A. Nygren, *Eros et Agapé*, Paris, 1951, vol. II, pp. 9-10).

Throughout the centuries, through many changes, the meaning of *eros* has been debased to merely sexual connotations. Characteristic, here, is the text of P. Chauchard, which even seems to deny *eros* the characteristics of human love:

"The cerebralization of sexuality does not lie in boring technical tricks, but in full recognition of its spirituality, since *Eros* is human only when it is animated by *Agapé* and since *Agapé* demands to be incarnated in *Eros*" (P. Chauchard, *Vices des vertus, vertus des vices*, Paris 1963, p. 147).

The comparison of biblical "knowledge" with Platonic *eros* reveals the divergence of these two concepts. The Platonic concept is based on nostalgia for transcendent Beauty and on escape from matter; the biblical concept, on the contrary, is geared to concrete reality, and the dualism of spirit and matter is alien to it as also the specific hostility to matter ("And God saw that it was good": Gn. 1:10, 12, 18, 21, 25).

Whereas the *Platonic* concept of *eros* goes beyond the biblical scope of human "knowledge," the *modern* concept seems *too restricted*. Biblical "knowledge" is not limited to satisfying instinct or hedonistic pleasure, but it is a fully human act, directed consciously towards procreation, and it is also the expression of interpersonal love (cf. Gn. 29:20; 1 Sm. 1:8; 2 Sm. 12:24).

Marriage in the
Integral Vision of Man

General audience of April 2, 1980.

Our meeting today takes place in the heart of Holy Week, on the immediate eve of that "Paschal Triduum," in which the whole liturgical year culminates and is illuminated. We are about to live again the decisive and solemn days, in which the work of human redemption was fulfilled: in them Christ, dying, destroyed our death and, rising again, restored life to us.

Each one must feel personally involved in the mystery that the liturgy, this year too, renews for us. I exhort you cordially, therefore, to take part with faith in the sacred services of the next few days and to commit yourselves in the determination to die to sin and to rise again ever more fully to the new life that Christ brought to us.

Let us resume, now, the treatment of the subject that has been occupying us for some time now.

1. The Gospel according to Matthew and the Gospel according to Mark report to us the answer given by Christ to the Pharisees, when they questioned Him about the indissolubility of marriage, referring to the law of Moses, which admitted, in certain cases, the practice of the so-called certificate of divorce. Reminding them of the first chapters of the Book of Genesis, Christ answered: "Have you not read that he who made them from the beginning made them male and female, and said, 'For this reason a man shall leave his father and mother and be joined to his wife, and the two shall become one flesh'? So they are no longer two but one flesh. What, therefore, God has joined together, let not man put asunder." Then, referring to their question about the law of Moses, Christ added: "For your hardness of heart Moses allowed you to divorce your wives, but from the beginning it was not so" (Mt. 19:3ff.; Mk. 12:2ff.). In His answer, Christ referred twice to the "beginning," and therefore we, too, in the course of our analyses, have tried to clarify in the deepest possible way the meaning of this "beginning," which is the first inheritance of every human being in the world, man and woman, the first attestation of human identity according to the revealed word, the first source of the certainty of man's vocation as a person created in the image of God Himself.

2. Christ's reply has a historical meaning—but not only a historical one. Men of all times raise the question on the same subject.

Our contemporaries, too, do so, but in their questions they do not refer to the law of Moses, which admitted the certificate of divorce, but to other circumstances and other laws. These questions of theirs are charged with problems, unknown to Christ's interlocutors. We know what questions concerning marriage and the family were addressed to the last Council, to Pope Paul VI, and are continually formulated in the post-conciliar period, day after day, in the most varied circumstances. They are addressed by single persons, married couples, fiancés, young people, but also by writers, journalists, politicians, economists, demographers, in a word, by contemporary culture and civilization.

I think that among the answers that Christ would give to the men of our time and to their questions, often so impatient, the one He gave to the Pharisees would still be fundamental. Answering those questions, Christ would refer above all to the "beginning." He would do so, perhaps, all the more resolutely and essentially in that the interior and at the same time cultural situation of modern man seems to be moving away from that "beginning" and assuming forms and dimensions which diverge from the biblical image of the "beginning" into points that are clearly more and more distant.

However, Christ would not be "surprised" by any of these situations, and I suppose that He would continue to refer mainly to the "beginning."

3. It was for this reason that Christ's answer called for a particularly thorough analysis. In that answer, in fact, fundamental and elementary truths about the human being, as man and woman, were recalled. It is the answer through which we catch a glimpse of the very structure of human identity in the dimensions of the mystery of creation and, at the same time, in the perspective of the mystery of redemption. Without that there is no way of constructing a theological anthropology and, in its context, a "theology of the body," from which also the view, fully Christian, of marriage and the family takes its origin. This was pointed out by Paul VI when, in his encyclical dedicated to the problems of marriage and procreation, in its responsible meaning on the human and Christian planes, he referred to the "total vision of man" *(Humanae vitae,* no. 7). It can be said that, in the answer to the Pharisees, Christ put forward to His interlocutors also this "total vision of man," without which no adequate answer can be given to questions connected with marriage and procreation. Precisely this total vision of man must be constructed from the "beginning."

This applies also to the modern mentality, just as it did, though in a different way, to Christ's interlocutors. We are, in fact, children of an age in which, owing to the development of various disciplines, this total vision of man may easily be rejected and replaced by multiple partial conceptions which, dwelling on one or other aspect of the *compositum humanum*, do not reach man's *integrum*, or leave it outside their own field of vision. Various cultural trends then take their place which—on the basis of these partial truths—formulate their proposals and practical indications on human behavior and, even more often, on how to behave with "man." Man then becomes more an object of determined techniques than the responsible subject of his own action. The answer given by Christ to the Pharisees also wishes man, male and female, to be this subject, that is, a subject who decides his own actions in the light of the complete truth about himself, since it is the original truth, or the foundation of genuinely human experiences. This is the truth that Christ makes us seek from the "beginning." Thus we turn to the first chapters of the Book of Genesis.

4. The study of these chapters, perhaps more than of others, makes us aware of the meaning and the necessity of the "theology of the body." The "beginning" tells us relatively little about the human body, in the naturalistic and modern sense of the word. From this point of view, in our study, we are at a completely pre-scientific level. We know hardly anything about the interior structures and the regularities that reign in the human organism. However, at the same time—perhaps precisely because of the antiquity of the text—the truth that is important for the total vision of man is revealed in the most simple and full way. This truth concerns

the meaning of the human body in the structure of the personal subject. Subsequently, reflection on those archaic texts enables us to extend this meaning of the whole sphere of human intersubjectivity, especially in the perennial man-woman relationship. Thanks to that, we acquire with regard to this relationship a perspective which we must necessarily place at the basis of all modern science on human sexuality, in the bio-physiological sense. That does not mean that we must renounce this science or deprive ourselves of its results. On the contrary: if the latter are to serve to teach us something about the education of man, in his masculinity and femininity, and about the sphere of marriage and procreation, it is necessary—through all the single· elements of contemporary science—always to arrive at what is fundamental and essentially personal, both in every individual, man or woman, and in their mutual relations.

And it is precisely at this point that reflection on the archaic text of Genesis is seen to be irreplaceable. It is really the "beginning" of the theology of the body. The fact that theology also considers the body should not astonish or surprise anyone who is aware of the mystery and reality of the Incarnation. Through the fact that the Word of God became flesh, the body entered theology—that is, the science, the subject of which is divinity, I would say—through the main door. The Incarnation—and the redemption that springs from it—became also the definitive source of the sacramentality of marriage, with which we will deal at greater length in due time.

5. The questions raised by modern man are also those of Christians: those who are preparing for the sacrament of marriage or those who are already living in marriage, which is the sacrament of the Church. These are not only the questions of science, but, even more, the questions of human life. So many men and so many Christians seek the accomplishment of their vocation in marriage. So many people wish to find in it the way to salvation and holiness.

The answer given by Christ to the Pharisees, zealots of the Old Testament, is particularly important for them. Those who seek the accomplishment of their own human and Christian vocation in marriage, are called, first of all, to make this "theology of the body," the "beginning" of which we find in the first chapters of the Book of Genesis, the content of their life and behavior. In fact, how indispensable is thorough knowledge of the meaning of the body, in its masculinity and femininity, along the way of this vocation! How necessary is a precise awareness of the nuptial meaning of the body, of its generating meaning—since all that which forms the content of the life of married couples must constantly find its full and personal dimension in life together, in behavior, in feelings! And all the more so against the background of a civilization which remains under the pressure of a materialistic and utilitarian way of thinking and evaluating. Modern bio-physiology can supply a great deal of precise information about human sexuality. However, knowledge of the personal dignity of the human body and of sex must still be drawn from other sources. A special source is the Word of God Himself, which contains the revelation of the body, going back to the "beginning."

How significant it is that Christ, in the answer to all these questions, orders man to return, in a way, to the threshold of his theological history! He orders him to put himself at the border between original innocence-happiness and the inheritance of the first fall. Does He not mean to tell him, perhaps, in this way, that the path along which He leads man, male-female, in the sacrament of marriage, that is, the path of the "redemption of the body," must consist in regaining this dignity in which there is accomplished, simultaneously, the real meaning of the human body, its personal meaning and its meaning "of communion"?

6. For the present, let us conclude the first part of our meditations dedicated to this important subject. To give an exhaustive answer to our questions, sometimes anxious ones, on marriage—or even more precisely: on the meaning of the body—we cannot dwell only on what Christ replied to the Pharisees, referring to the "beginning" (cf. Mt. 19:3ff.; Mk. 10:2ff.). We must also take into consideration all His other statements, of which two, of a particularly comprehensive character, emerge especially: the

first one, from the Sermon on the Mount, on the possibilities of the human heart in relation to the lust of the body (cf. Mt. 5:8), and the second one, when Jesus referred to the future resurrection (cf. Mt. 22:24-30; Mk. 12:18-27; Lk. 20:27-36).

We intend to make these two statements the subject of our following reflections.*

---

*Inquire about the subsequent volumes on catechesis on the Sermon on the Mount and catechesis on the Letters of St. Paul available from the Daughters of St. Paul (addresses at the end of this book).

INDEX

Also available from St. Paul Editions:

BOOKS

An Augustine Treasury

Edited by Jules M. Brady, S.J.

Selections from the writings of St. Augustine covering a wide range of subjects such as God, creation, sin, grace, heaven, happiness, the meaning of life, Christian virtues, the Church, and the sacraments.

212 pages   cloth $3.95   paper $2.95 — FA0015

Declaration on Certain Questions Concerning Sexual Ethics

Sacred Congregation for the Doctrine of the Faith

"...The purpose of this Declaration is to draw the attention of the faithful in present-day circumstances to certain errors and modes of behavior which they must guard against."

27 pages   20¢ — PM0500

Lifetime of Love

S.L. Hart

The practical problems of everyday family living. Backed by the sound doctrine of Vatican II. Covers the whole span of married life—from the day of the wedding until "sunset." Newlyweds, in-laws, the budget, raising children, sex instruction for little ones, divorce, birth control, family cooperation, the role of mother and father, teenagers, growing old together—these and countless more topics in this complete, up-to-date marriage manual.

534 pages   cloth $5.95 — MS0350

The Lord of History

Msgr. Eugene Kevane

"This is an excellent introduction to the Christian philosophy of history—clearly written, comprehensive

within the limits of its less than 200 pages, and cognizant of the important modern issues." (From a review by James Hitchcock, Fellowship of Catholic Scholars.)
200 pages   cloth $4.00   paper $3.00 — RA0135

Remarried Divorcees and Eucharistic Communion

Rev. Bertrand de Margerie, S.J.

This book examines the problem from a solid scriptural basis, within the context of both the Old and New Testaments, and traces the clear and unbroken line of doctrinal teaching on this subject down the centuries, from the Fathers of the Church to post-Tridentine theologians.
112 pages   cloth $3.00   paper $1.95 — MS0593

Sexual Inversion: The Questions—
With Catholic Answers

Rev. Herbert F. Smith, S.J., with Joseph A. Di Ienno, M.D. Introduction by V. Michael Vaccaro, M.D.

Informative treatment of such topics as: Homosexuality, morality, and religion; homosexuality and the medical sciences; homosexuality and society; living with one's homosexual orientation.
cloth $2.95   paper $1.95 — RA0165

U.S.A.—The Message of Justice, Peace and Love

Pope John Paul II
Compiled and indexed by the Daughters of St. Paul

Complete collection of the talks given by His Holiness during his historic visit to America, October 1-7, 1979: Boston, New York, Philadelphia, Des Moines, Chicago, Washington.

What did the Vicar of Christ tell America wherever he went? A book to treasure, to meditate, to live by.
320 pages   cloth $5.95   paper $4.95 — EP1095

Vatican Council II—The Conciliar and Post-Conciliar Documents

General Editor—Austin Flannery, O.P.

"The need for the book is crucial, not only for readers of English but for scholars generally.... The

compendium is a unique collection of translations into English of Council documents, together with selected subsequent Roman documents which amplify, elucidate, or apply the major themes of the Vatican Council constitutions, decrees, and other major pronouncements..." (John Cardinal Wright).
1062 pages   paper $4.95 — EP1097

The Whole Truth About Man

Pope John Paul II
Edited and with an introduction by Rev. James V. Schall, S.J.
Indexed by the Daughters of St. Paul
      The Holy Father's talks to university faculties and students.
354 pages   cloth $7.95   paper $6.95 — EP1099

Yes to Life

Edited by the Daughters of St. Paul
      An invaluable source-book bringing together the consistent teaching of the Church through the centuries on the sacredness of human life.
      Here in one volume is proclaimed the fundamental truth of the value of all human life in the words of the Fathers of the Church, the Popes, Vatican II and the bishops of our day.
330 pages   cloth $6.95   paper $5.95 — EP1110

PAMPHLETS

Conscience and Morality

      A doctrinal statement of the Irish Episcopal Conference.
30 pages   50¢ — PM0457

Marriage and Family Life

Most. Rev. Justin A. Driscoll
      A pastoral letter on the topic.
30 pages   35¢ — PM1215

On Jesus Christ Our Redeemer (Tametsi Futura Prospicientibus)

Pope Leo XIII
    November 1, 1900.
22 pages   40¢ — EP0679

On the Mercy of God (Dives in Misericordia)

Pope John Paul II
52 pages   50¢ — EP0863

Pastoral Letter on Homosexuality

Most. Rev. John R. Quinn,
    Archbishop of San Francisco
22 pages   25¢ — PM1536

Pastoral Reflections on Conscience

Humberto Cardinal Medeiros
12 pages   20¢ — PM1443

Religious Freedom and the Dignity of Woman

Marina E. Ruffolo
    A penetrating study of the true value of each individual, which emphasizes the person's relationship to God as the basis of human dignity.
32 pages   75¢ — PM1615

Something Worth Celebrating

John Cardinal Wright
    Reflections on the beauty of Christian family life.
22 pages   25¢ — PM1802

Inquire about The Family *for the home and* My Friend *for children—two magazines that instill lasting family values.*

Please order from addresses on the following page, specifying title and item number.

Daughters of St. Paul

IN MASSACHUSETTS
  50 St. Paul's Ave. Jamaica Plain, Boston, MA 02130;
    617-522-8911; 617-522-0875;
  172 Tremont Street, Boston, MA 02111; **617-426-5464;**
    617-426-4230
IN NEW YORK
  78 Fort Place, Staten Island, NY 10301; **212-447-5071**
  59 East 43rd Street, New York, NY 10017; **212-986-7580**
  7 State Street, New York, NY 10004; **212-447-5071**
  625 East 187th Street, Bronx, NY 10458; **212-584-0440**
  525 Main Street, Buffalo, NY 14203; **716-847-6044**
IN NEW JERSEY
  Hudson Mall — Route 440 and Communipaw Ave.,
    Jersey City, NJ 07304; **201-433-7740**
IN CONNECTICUT
  202 Fairfield Ave., Bridgeport, CT 06604; **203-335-9913**
IN OHIO
  2105 Ontario St. (at Prospect Ave.), Cleveland, OH 44115; **216-621-9427**
  25 E. Eighth Street, Cincinnati, OH 45202; **513-721-4838**
IN PENNSYLVANIA
  1719 Chestnut Street, Philadelphia, PA 19103; **215-568-2638**
IN FLORIDA
  2700 Biscayne Blvd., Miami, FL 33137; **305-573-1618**
IN LOUISIANA
  4403 Veterans Memorial Blvd., Metairie, LA 70002; **504-887-7631;**
    504-887-0113
  1800 South Acadian Thruway, P.O. Box 2028, Baton Rouge, LA 70821
    504-343-4057; 504-343-3814
IN MISSOURI
  1001 Pine Street (at North 10th), St. Louis, MO 63101; **314-621-0346;**
    314-231-1034
IN ILLINOIS
  172 North Michigan Ave., Chicago, IL 60601; **312-346-4228;**
    312-346-3240
IN TEXAS
  114 Main Plaza, San Antonio, TX 78205; **512-224-8101**
IN CALIFORNIA
  1570 Fifth Avenue, San Diego, CA 92101; **714-232-1442**
  46 Geary Street, San Francisco, CA 94108; **415-781-5180**
IN HAWAII
  1143 Bishop Street, Honolulu, HI 96813; **808-521-2731**
IN ALASKA
  750 West 5th Avenue, Anchorage AK 99501; **907-272-8183**
IN CANADA
  3022 Dufferin Street, Toronto 395, Ontario, Canada
IN ENGLAND
  128, Notting Hill Gate, London W11 3QG, England
  133 Corporation Street, Birmingham B4 6PH, England
  5A-7 Royal Exchange Square, Glasgow G1 3AH, England
  82 Bold Street, Liverpool L1 4HR, England
IN AUSTRALIA
  58 Abbotsford Rd., Homebush, N.S.W., Sydney 2140, Australia